Robert Rhea: The Johannine Son of Man

Robert Rhea

The Johannine Son of Man

WIPF & STOCK · Eugene, Oregon

Wipf and Stock Publishers
199 W 8th Ave, Suite 3
Eugene, OR 97401

The Johannine Son of Man
By Rhea, Robert
Copyright© by Rhea, Robert
ISBN 13: 978-1-5326-3703-2

Publication date 8/31/2017
Previously published by Theologischer Verlag Zürich, 1990

To all those who from even before the
time of Abraham and Sarah to the day
of Jesus of Galilee, the Messiah, the
Anointed One of Israel, until the present have lived on this earth the life
of a child of humankind.

CONTENTS

	Preface to the 2017 Reprint Edition	5
	Preface	9
I	Introduction	11
II	Johannine Language and Apocalyptic Vision	21
	A The Apocalyptic View of the World	24
	B The Synoptic Logia	27
	C Three Johannine Sayings	32
	1) John 5,27	32
	2) John 6,62	39
	3) John 9,35	43
III	The Prophet	49
	A John 6,53	49
	B Cullmann's Heavenly Man	57
IV	Conclusion	69
	Notes to the Text	72
	Bibliography	76

Preface to the 2017 Reprint Edition

During the autumn of 1978 I first made a formal, exegetical presentation of the Johannine, prophetic Son of Man with a seminar paper for James L. Martyn at Union Theological Seminary, New York. I contended then as I do now that the use of the Son of Man title in the Fourth Gospel betrays a definite revelatory tradition related directly to the tradition of Hebrew prophecy; and that though the scriptural basis for this view is sparsely attested in both the Greek and Hebrew Scriptures, it can nonetheless be documented with biblical texts which provide both spiritual and theological sources. Prior to that semester I had completed a lecture course on the Fourth Gospel taught by Raymond E. Brown for which I wrote a paper on the Paraclete.

Two primary observations emerged from these learning experiences. First of all, considering the spirituality presented in the first three chapters of the Fourth Gospel, it became clear to me that the spirituality of this Gospel is firmly grounded in the dream and vision cycles of the Hebrew Bible, i.e., as stated above, in the revelatory theophanies of the Hebrew prophets and prophetesses. Secondly it became abundantly evident that these two professors, whose personalities were as different as night and day, approached the Fourth Gospel from contradictory points of view. Martyn, who was by confession a Protestant, asserted that the so-called dualism and the bitter polemic against some of the Jewish people and non-Christians recorded here had come about as a result of the social conflicts that arose as the Johannine Christians were expelled from the synagogue (Birkat ha-Minim from the Council of Jamnia). Brown was an ordained Roman Catholic priest and a member of a French academic order, whose extraordinary commentary demonstrated that this Gospel had evolved over the course of the first century from unique Johannine as well as Synoptic sources (he posited the existence of a second Synoptic source) as the Johannine community emerged with a more mature view of Jesus' *kerygma*. I hoped that I could provide a way to overcome this divisiveness with my paper on the Son of Man, for I was convinced that it mirrored the Hebrew spirituality that undergirded the Johannine account of the teaching and life of Jesus of Galilee.

Prior to the Son of Man paper, my discussions with both of these professors was centered primarily on the exegesis of chapter three of the Fourth Gospel, particularly John 3:13. I argued that one is dealing here with a heavenly Son of Man, a Hebrew version of Cullmann's Original or Heavenly Man: "No one has ascended into heaven but the one who has descended from heaven, even the Son of Man who is in heaven."[1] Jesus' reply to Nicodemus' query takes up the theme of heavenly but personal revelation, John 3:3b: "Turly, truly I say to you, unless one is begotten from above, one cannot see the kingdom of God." I am rather certain that John 3:13 addresses this, for it seems clear that Jesus adds this assertion to his earlier reply. Thus Nicodemus will not ascend into heaven, unless he himself also descends from heaven, i.e., he must be renewed and enlivened personally by the Divine Presence, which has its origin in and comes from heaven. This concept is further explained and complemented by John 6:53–54 and 6:62–63. Here it is clear that Jesus is saying that he as Son of Man made himself known from heaven before he came to earth and that after his death he will return to that divine place which is his home. Thus it is only the human perception of his heavenly spiritual presence that reveals to those in the earthly realm the true spirituality of salvation.

Yet both Martyn and Brown rejected such a proposal with the argument that here the Fourth Evangelist is concerned with the polemic centered on the mythological legends of Enoch and Elijah who did not die but were reportedly translated into heaven, rising somehow from the earth as they flew into heaven. They maintained that on the contrary only Jesus descended from heaven and that later after his death only he ascended into heaven. No one else but he has accomplished this, and thus the salvation of all humankind is ultimately based on this divine event.

---

1. This reading is attested by the manuscript Alexandrinus from the fifth century AD and by six other manuscripts which date from the eight to ninth centuries AD.

Preface to the 2017 Reprint Edition

I countered their argument with the assertion that they were reading this verse and others from the Fourth Gospel, such as John 3:16, from a Pauline perspective. For Paul, only Jesus died and rose from the dead. His view of salvation is centered on the vicarious suffering of Jesus on the cross and thus Christians have come to substitute his death and resurrection for the concept of the Incarnation of the Hebrew God, which the Fourth Evangelist presents in the first chapter. Not only is Jesus the Hebrew God Incarnate who has descended from and who has ascended into heaven, all believers both before and after Jesus' day who have apprehended the Divine Presence spiritually, and some who have had dreams and visions, have also descended from and ascended into heaven.

Robert Rhea
May, 2017
Bristol, Tennessee

Preface

The Son of Man riddle continues to be one of the most challenging and baffling aspects of the Christian faith. Although some scholars are no longer convinced of its importance and have relegated it to a peripheral role in Christ's teachings, a good number of other scholars are certain that the title has a central role to play in interpreting Jesus' messianic mission. For centuries it has been ignored, and there is substantial evidence which indicates that even the primitive church of the first century did not fully understand its significance or use it consistently as a messianic title. Its definite Semitic character as well as the possibility of a Hebrew equivalent suggest that it could well serve to minimize the great, controversial differences between the Jewish and Christian understanding of the Hebrew scriptures.

When I began my formal study of the Gospel of John ten years ago, I was convinced that the Evangelist's concept of spirituality was a constant. I first wrote on the role of the Paraclete because I was certain that although that term was introduced only at the end of the Gospel, its presence could be discerned in a flowing continuum from the Baptism to the crucifixion. Yet after I finished that presentation, I was not satisfied that I had isolated the basic, underlying concept of the Johannine understanding of Hebrew spirituality. It was then that I cast my gaze on the term Son of Man and decided that it played the key role. It is my opinion that an appropriate, contemporary translation of the term might well be child of humankind. To my ears that expression has a timeless, joyful, innocent ring to it. My hope is that others might also perceive that quality about it.

I would like to thank a host of friends, professors, and ministers for sharing with me their views on this topic. I have spent many hours with them engaged in delightful conversations about scripture as well as the joys and sorrows of attempting to be a Christian in this age of turmoil and debate. The assistance of Dr. Richard Ray, Dr. Frank Thielman, and Dr. Willis Wager who generously helped with the task of editing has been greatly appreciated. To Dr. Erich Graesser and Dr. Oscar Cullmann I wish to extend my most heartfelt regards and thank them so very much for their encouragement and their help in making the publication of this project possible. I look forward to the opportunity of continuing correspondence with them. Finally, I would like to thank my father, mother, and sister for their assistance and patience. They have been somewhat reluctant yet very willing to tolerate the life of a wandering Christian. May they understand that this has not been a matter of choice.

August 11, 1988   Robert Rhea

Bristol, Tennessee U.S.A.

I Introduction

The perplexing Son of Man debate continues to challenge and stimulate those who choose to turn to the subject matter with the tools of modern exegesis. A wealth of literature has been dedicated to the project; and yet despite the efforts of a great number of contributors, there is perhaps less agreement on the matter today than ever before. As R. H. Fuller has recently stated, "It is notorious that there are almost as many opinions about the Son of Man as there are scholars who deal with it."[1] Another scholar, baffled by the fact that the results of the research are so varied and often far-fetched, has expressed his doubt that even a partial solution to the debate can be achieved unless a new and fresh approach is discovered.

Indeed Jesus' use of the term Son of Man has been and continues to be one of the supreme riddles of the New Testament κήρυγμα. In the attempt to unravel the Son of Man mystery scholars have rummaged through thousands of ancient texts of the Ancient Near East ranging from the writings of Plato to the recently discovered Ras Shamra texts. The use of the term as a messianic title in the Synoptics, the Gospel of John, and in Acts 7,56 blatantly disrupts the pristine order generated by a host of other more accepted titles and serves to create a definite sense of incongruity in the regular sayings of Jesus. The effect of its use is so mysterious and dominant that it is hard to avoid the likely presupposition that even during Jesus' day and during the time of the primitive Church it must have been an enigmatic term. It is very probable, therefore, that Jesus himself intended it to be an unsettling and radical designation, yet at the same time found it a fitting and appropriate means of expressing his sonship to God.

Introduction

The center of the debate has been focused on the Synoptic logia, since it has been assumed that they are the earliest and most authentic sayings. For these reasons the Johannine logia have been neglected by those who have entered the mainstream of the debate. Those who have turned to the use of the term Son of Man in John have sought to show first and foremost that the Fourth Evangelist derived the core of his sayings from an earlier, traditional source utilized also by the other evangelists, and then proceeded to mold these original sayings to fit a more sober and mature Christian world-view which emerged at the end of the first century. The source of the debate, however, is the same in both arenas. What was the original <u>Sitz im Leben</u> of the term and how has it been edited to provide for a meaningful and integral theme of Jesus' message? Here the crucial matter of concern has been the extent to which the term can be viewed to be an apocalyptic designation or title. Did in fact Jesus or the primitive community take the title along with its underlying concept directly from the works of Jewish apocalyptic literature, specifically Dan. 7,13? To what extent is it possible that the term and its titular use arose out of the crosscurrents of the traditions and legends of the Primal Man which have been documented in Judaism, numerous religions of the Ancient Near East, and Hellenistic philosophy? Finally, it is also probable that the term serves simply as a circumlocution for the personal pronoun "I," or that it is merely a self-designation or a self-reference which Jesus himself coined from the Aramaism.

Despite the debate on these questions, however, it has generally been accepted that the Synoptic title has been derived from a consistent, unified concept of the heavenly, transcendent Redeemer who is depicted in the Jewish apocalyptic literature. Although modern scholarship has successfully refuted Bultmann on a host of major issues of interpretation, because he too held that the title had its origins in Jewish apocalyptic, Son of Man Christology is one area where his influence has left its mark on a num-

Introduction

ber of subsequent studies. By attributing the formation of the majority of the Son of Man logia to the initiative of the ecclesiastical redactor, he divorced the use of the title from the central core of the κήρυγμα and regarded it primarily as the fruit of Jesus' attempt to incorporate a popular myth into his teaching. According to Bultmann Jesus could have spoken only of a future Son of Man who was to come at the end of time but who was a transcendent figure other than himself. From this assessment of the matter it is only a small step away to the startling view of Philipp Vielhauer that since with one exception there is no evidence in the Synoptics that Jesus ever spoke of the Son of Man in direct relationship to the dominant theme of his preaching, the coming of the Kingdom of God, and since it is certain that Jesus preached the coming of the Kingdom, it is obvious that he never spoke of the Son of Man at all.[2]

The work of H. E. Toedt betrays the influence of these viewpoints. Agreeing with Bultmann and Bousset that it was psychologically impossible for Jesus to have claimed to be a "super-terrestrial, transcendent Messiah or even a future Son of Man designate,"[3] he points to the emphasis on the authority and sovereignty of the apocalyptic Son of Man who is regarded as the future, transcendent figure who is to vindicate Jesus and his teaching at the last judgment. Toedt, however, is much more interested in the early church than the authentic sayings of Jesus, and proceeds to document the process whereby the early church read the title back into the earthly ministry of Jesus to provide for the divine validation of the earthly authority of Jesus. In doing so the early church discarded the apocalyptic trappings of the transcendent Son of Man and developed essentially two Christologies. Mark and Paul understand Jesus according to their conception of a passion κήρυγμα evolving from Phil. 2,5-11, Mk. 10,45 and Mk. 14,24. Q, on the other hand, sees Jesus primarily as the authoritative teacher and looks to the resurrection for the validation of Jesus' earthly authority.[4]

Introduction

Higgins' theory is very similar to that of Toedt. It is his opinion that only the future sayings can be considered to be authentic. Though he chooses to incorporate the Johannine sayings into the discussion, he quickly abandons them as being irrelevant for any determination of the teachings of the historical Jesus. Agreeing with Toedt on the significance of Dan. 7, 13, he points out that Jesus did not refer directly to that passage during the course of his initial teaching, but asserts that Jesus later adapted it "to denote himself as the Son of God he already believed himself to be."[5] Whereas Bultmann and his school differentiate between Jesus and the future Son of Man, he holds the view that Jesus actually looked to a time in the future when he would perform Son of Man functions. It was for this reason that the early church thought of Jesus as the Son of Man.[6]

The work of E. Stauffer points to the beginnings of the attempt to greatly minimize the influence of an apocalyptic Son of Man on the teachings of Jesus. Although in his early work he agrees that Jesus knowingly assumed the use of the title and grants that almost all of the Synoptic sayings are authentic, in his later work he becomes very suspicious of the presence of actual apocalyptic elements in the teachings of Jesus and disclaims the authenticity of all the future sayings.[7] Likewise Eduard Schweizer takes a stand against the popular views of the German school. He also rejects the authenticity of all of the future, apocalyptic Son of Man sayings on the grounds that the term Son of Man originally referred to the Jewish concept of the humiliated, vindicated, and finally exalted suffering, righteous man. Pointing to Wisdom 2-5, Enoch 70-71, Dodd's assessment of Ps. 80 and 8, Paul, and Acts 7,56, Schweizer carefully lays out his theory that the New Testament concept of the vindicated Son of Man was developed along the lines of the exalted and glorified Righteous One who is seated on the throne of the heavenly court at the last judgment rather than an apocalyptic Son of Man who was to come to earth at the end of time. Because the Jewish literature

Introduction

points up the integral relationship between the lowly, rejected, and humiliated suffering servant of righteousness and his subsequent exaltation and glorification, Schweizer finds those sayings which depict the earthly life of Jesus to be the most authentic. Convinced that the traditional theme of the exaltation which is evident in Acts 7,56 can also be uncovered in the Johannine sayings, he demonstrates how the Fourth Evangelist has emphatically related the task of the lowly servant to the concept of glorification and his supreme role in the heavenly court at the last judgment. "Das Besondere dieser Tradition liegt aber darin, dass trotzdem der auf Erden wandelnde Menschensohn im Brennpunkt des Interesses steht."[8]

The work of C. Colpe sees New Testament Son of Man Christology as a phenomenon which has been derived from an early, Jewish-Christian theology of which there remain no records except a few, early Synoptic logia. He rules out the possibility that the title could have evolved out of Judaism, excludes also all of the Jewish apocalyptic literature, and claims that the Ras Shamra texts are the only, likely, non-Israelite source of the formative, mythological concept. The works of Daniel, I Enoch, and IV Ezra provide knowledge of a few of the groups who awaited a messianic Son of Man. However, they present only literary reflections of some of the possible expectations these groups developed, not a single system of Jewish, apocalyptic theology in which the expectation of the Son of Man functioned as a specific concept and title. Yet from a fourth source a specific Son of Man concept did emerge which contained the expectation of an earthly parousia and which Jesus used as the basis for eight authentic, future sayings. From this point on Colpe's work resembles that of Toedt as he proceeds to document the formation of the other sayings within the confines of the primitive communities.[9]

It was apparently findings like those reported by Schweizer and Colpe which inspired Norman Perrin to examine the Jewish apocalyptic literature

Introduction

and announce his startling discovery that with regard to the term Son of Man in ancient Judaism and primitive Christianity "there is no 'Son of Man concept' but rather a variety of uses of Son of Man imagery."[10] Above all, Perrin is confident that a single, unified, pre-Christian concept of a transcendent, apocalyptic Son of Man who was to judge the world at the beginning of the Second Aeon never existed. The Jewish and Christian concepts of the "cloud man" were developed exegetically yet independent of one another in both the Rabbinic and Christian traditions, evolving via Dan. 7,13 through I Enoch, IV Ezra, and Psalms 2,9; 21,5; and 110,1. Perrin argues that if there were such a concept, the redemptive and eschatological authority of the figure would rest solely on the sense of apocalyptic pre-existence attributed to the Son of Man figure. Because, however, pre-existence is an essential element of the apocalyptic drama commonly ascribed to all of its major figures(the Saints of the Most High, the Ancient of Days etc.), he rejects the notion that this one point will validate the authority of a definite Son of Man concept in Jewish apocalyptic. Neither the midrashic nor the Christian tradition was wholly indebted to Jewish apocalyptic for the concept which eventually emerged. There were, therefore, no apocalyptic Son of Man sayings in the teaching of Jesus; and the identification of Jesus as the Son of Man in the dominical logia cannot be considered as a basis for the beginning of Christology.[11]

Impressed by the absence of the Similitudes of Enoch at Qumran, Ragnar Leivestad also holds the view that no definite, apocalyptic Son of Man title can be documented on the basis of Jewish apocalyptic literature and the earliest logia of the primitive Christian communities. He differs from Perrin on the origin and early use of the term, however, for he finds it to be essentially a self-reference which Jesus used to refer ambiguously to his own humanity on the one hand and his messianic role as a representative of humanity on the other. He agrees with Schweizer that the most authentic

Introduction

sayings are those in which Jesus speaks of himself as the lowly, earthly Son of Man. He does not concede the possibility that the term may have been used as a circumlocution for the personal pronoun "I," but rather suggests that it eventually came to be viewed as his popular name. Leivestad also considers it likely that Jesus thought of himself as Ezekiel redivivus.[12]

R. H. Fuller rejects Perrin's theory that the independent pesher interpretation of Dan. 7,13 accounts for the origin of the earthly Son of Man sayings as well as many of the future sayings. Instead he turns to the philological argument to postulate the use of the bar nasha idiom as a self-reference in spite of the lack of evidence in the Aramaic use of the term at the time of Jesus. Fuller proceeds to posit two primary stages of the "self-effacing, self-referent" bar nasha, neither of which led to the titular use of the term. He asserts that when the early church developed the pesher Son of Man sayings based on Dan. 7,13, it still continued to regard the term as a non-titular self-referent. Although Jesus was made to speak of himself as the one who would come on the clouds as a judge at the end of time, nevertheless he was never regarded as an apocalyptic figure. Unlike Perrin, Fuller thus avoids the dilemma created by the unlikely possibility that both the later midrashic, apocalyptic tradition of Rabbinic Judaism and the Christian tradition could have developed independently and simultaneously a future, apocalyptic Son of Man concept. He contends that in Jewish apocalyptic the term initially functioned as a definite title for the eschatological judge and savior.[13]

In his latest work on the topic Barnabas Lindars avails himself of the use of the philological source of the term, and strictly rules out the possibility that it occurs as an apocalyptic title in Daniel and the other works of Jewish apocalyptic literature. Citing the detailed findings of Lietzmann, Dalman, Vermes and others, Lindars weaves his own knowledge of the Hebrew and Aramaic background into the argument and demonstrates that

Introduction

the term has originally been derived from an idiomatic, Aramaic self-referent which successfully preserves a generic meaning. Thus Jesus actually used the idiom in an oblique way to refer to himself. He can never have intended to identify himself as the Danielic Son of Man, since "according to the Jewish evidence for this usage, he must have spoken generically."[14] Lindars, therefore, makes the claim that only those Son of Man sayings which preserve the Aramaic idiom can be considered authentic. Altogether he finds nine sayings in Mark and Q which retain the idiom. Six of these are present sayings of the earthly Jesus, while another three have been isolated among the passion predictions. According to Lindars the titular usage found in all the other sayings is a later formation which resulted either when the term was translated into Greek or when at a much later time Dan. 7,13 was viewed by the early church from a christological perspective.[15]

The absence of the typical, Synoptic, apocalyptic imagery which usually accompanies the term Son of Man is a striking feature of the Gospel of John, and the determination of the influence of eschatology and apocalyptic on this gospel is of crucial importance. The prominence of the assumed apocalyptic title in the Johannine sayings has led most scholars to conclude that it can have been derived from no other source than Jewish apocalyptic. Even those who expound the view that the term and concept originated in the Hebrew scriptures and that the Johannine Son of Man concept has been derived from the Jewish concept of the ideal Man(Borsch, Sidebottom, Smalley, Schulz, Ricca) see Jewish apocalyptic as a dominant force which has molded and shaped the term prior to its appearance in the Synoptic logia. On the other hand, those who assert that the apocalyptic concept has been recast and redefined according to the dictates of the Hellenistic ideal Man(Dodd, Lightfoot, Hamerton-Kelley) continue to view apocalyptic as the setting which gave rise to the expression. This is also the

Introduction

opinion of those scholars who find that the original apocalyptic title has been reshaped to provide for a metamorphosis of its essential character, enabling it to present a completely new concept(Kinniburgh, Meeks, Martyn). Finally, there are some who hold the view that John's use of the Son of Man title transcends the accepted christological concept such that it has become a virtual equivalent for the concept of Logos or the title, Son of God.

Francis Moloney has presented an excellent review of the Johannine Son of Man debate up until 1975 in the first chapter of his comprehensive study of the function of the title in John's Gospel. A survey of that material reveals that no one has sought to relate the Johannine debate to that arena of Synoptic concern which has challenged the theory of the apocalyptic source for the title. Even Moloney whose study provides a significant, new insight into the specific function of the title in John refuses to consider the possibility of a non-apocalyptic origin: "Yet it could equally be argued that the figure which was promised in Dan. 7 and applied to Jesus in the Synoptic tradition stands behind John's use of the title."[16] The prominence of this opinion is particularly striking when one considers the fact that some scholars find the Johannine logia to be as old as the Synoptic sayings and think that they may have been derived from an Aramaic source preserved by the primitive community(Smalley). In light of the new evidence that there was no consistent, apocalyptic Son of Man concept operative in ancient Judaism and considering the fact that the Johannine logia may well be based on authentic sayings of Jesus, the theory that the Johannine use of the title may have been derived from a non-apocalyptic source becomes very plausible. Such a theory would help to explain the Johannine phenomenon of "realized eschatology" as well as the lack of Synoptic, apocalyptic elements in the Son of Man sayings and in the gospel as a whole. This would not mean that the Evangelist has refused to incorporate

19

Introduction

into his work the essential, eschatological elements of the Christian κήρυγμα. It would mean only that he has taken his eschatological worldview from a source other than that of Jewish apocalyptic.

II Johannine Language and Apocalyptic Vision

Rudolf Otto was convinced that I Enoch established a mythological, messianic pattern according to which Jesus proclaimed himself to be the Son of Man. He asserts that Jesus' use of the term authenticates his teachings of the Kingdom of God and validates his claim to be the Messiah: "That Christ himself held his own knowledge of God to be unique and incomparable is proved by the bold words with which he placed himself high above the revelation given through the prophets and the wisdom of antiquity: 'Here is more than Jonah and Solomon.' "[17]

Otto was a speculative syncretist who held the view that Jesus' concept of the Kingdom of God and the Son of Man title has non-Israelite origins in the ancient religions and mythologies of Persia and India, all of which in his opinion were based on the Asura religion. His work parallels the more recent study of F. Borsch who is certain that the apocalyptic Son of Man and the Jewish concept of the Messiah are rooted in the myths of the Primal Man of the Ancient Near East and the kingship rites of ancient Babylon, Canaan, and Israel. Colpe has denied that the apocalyptic Son of Man concept can be traced to Iranian, Babylonian, Egyptian, Rabbinic or gnostic sources. He also disclaims any relationship between the Aramaism and its Hebrew counterpart found in Ezekiel and the Psalms. He admits only one possibility for the non-Israelite source of the term which is "the mythological similarity between the relation of the Ancient of Days and the Son of Man on the one side and that of El and Baal on the other"[18] which has come to light as the result of the deciphering of the Ras Shamra texts of Canaanite origin. Colpe warns, however, that no direct relation-

Johannine Language and Apocalyptic Vision

ship can be presupposed and that the myth itself is concerned with "the depiction of an appearance, ...not the adoption of the term 'man.' "[19]

In the face of Colpe's objective pessimism on the one hand and the unrealistic, speculative, and subjective enthusiasm of Otto and Borsch on the other, it appears that a more sober, realistic middle ground might be reached. No one can deny that the term Son of Man has a mysterious quality about it which echoes out of the distant reaches of the past. The fact that it has been remarkably and yet paradoxically couched in the bold language of John's account of the Eucharist suggests that it must have had a broader sphere of reference than that of Jewish apocalyptic. J. L. Martyn indicates that he is very much aware of this dimension of the debate when he observes that on four occasions John's presentation of the title follows at the end of a midrashic discussion of Jesus' teachings during the course of which Jesus is at first identified as the Mosaic-Prophet-Messiah. The work of Herbert Leroy which demonstrates that the Evangelist has patterned the Gospel after the format of the literary genre of the riddle prevalent in the Ancient Near East is signigicant in this regard also. According to his findings one can assume that the Gospel of John is a long riddle comprised of concepts, phrases, and episodes whose meaning is known only to the inner circle of believers. It is clear that the term Son of Man has a precise meaning and that the Evangelist deems it a matter of the utmost importance that Jesus be designated not only as the Messiah, the Mosaic Prophet, the King of Israel, the Son of God, and the Savior of the World but also most emphatically the Son of Man.

With regard to the philological argument it must be objected that Lindars has no definite basis on which to rest his claim that Jesus can never have used the Aramaism titularly. It is true that Vermes asserts that his work vindicates Lietzmann's original theory "that no Aramaic-speaking person would ever have used 'Son of Man' as a title."[20] Examining the term in

Rabbinic passages which include the Geniza fragments and the Neofiti Codex, Vermes shows that bar nash occurs "with a generic meaning, an indefinite meaning, as a substitute for 'I.'"[21] Yet he also points out "that the speaker, when referring to himself, may make this explicit by the use of in the definite form, i.e., with the definite article, bar nasha, the one you know."[22]

Thus what Lindars considers only an idiomatic, generic use of the article may in fact be a definite form, referring explicitly to the speaker only. Black concedes that there was no evidence for a title in the Aramaic passages which Vermes consulted, yet asserts "that does not mean that the term was incapable of becoming a title."[23] As Colpe has indicated, all four terms of the idiom appear to have been interchangeable in Jesus' time. Yet C. F. D. Moule's observation is certainly worthy of note: "Where the phrase ' 'o uios tou anthropou' is related to Jesus, it is, with almost complete consistency, the form with the definite article/11/."[24] According to Black the following assertion can be made: "This suggests that all genuine 'Son of Man' sayings go back to an original bar nasha= 'the Son of Man,' the one you know."[25] In any event the Greek expression itself points strongly to the Semitic(Hebrew/Aramaic) term both with regard to its form and content. The idiom must be understood as an ambiguous designation which Jesus could have used as a generic self-referent or as a title.

Nevertheless, Lindars' position does rest on a considerable amount of evidence which is in his favor. The Synoptic logia in particular lend credence to the possibility that Jesus alternated in his use of the term, using it interchangeably as an idiom with a definite generic sense and also as a specific title. Perhaps the most obvious example of this usage is Mt. 16,13: "Who do men say that the Son of Man is?" Here it could well be argued that the term was not originally intended as a messianic title. If, however, the term was an actual messianic title, what was the essential

The Apocalyptic View of the World

nature of the titular designation which prompted Jesus to use it also in a generic fashion?

A The Apocalyptic View of the World

There can be little doubt about the fact that much of the imagery which accompanies the Synoptic Son of Man figure has been taken from the apocalyptic works of Daniel, I Enoch, and IV Ezra. In the early church Jesus is identified with the pre-existent, transcendent figure who resembles a man and who is exalted by God to judge the world and vindicate the righteous at the end of time. Yet the Synoptic view of this event is a confused one and does not consistently reflect the visionary imagery and the symbology of the apocalyptic accounts.

Concerning the dates of these works, it is certain that the Danielic account of the vision is the oldest. It must have been composed sometime between 200-165 B.C. The date for the writing of the Similitudes of Enoch continues to be a source for controversy, primarily because of the mysterious absence of this work at Qumran where all other portions of I Enoch were discovered. Since they contain verbal parallels to Mt. 25,31 and Jn. 5,22 and 27, Charles insists on giving it a date as early as the first half of the last century B.C. Others, however, are very skeptical about such an early date. Knibb proposes the end of the first century A.D., while Milik even considers the end of the third century A.D. As for IV Ezra there seems to be little doubt that it is a much later work dating from the end of the first century A.D.

The argument that both Dan. 7 and the Similitudes of Enoch can be traced to the kingship ceremonies of Babylonian and Canaanite mythology is well-known and has been mentioned above. The similarity of the Israelite Enthronement Festival to the myth and ritual pattern of these ceremonies

of the Ancient Near East has attracted the interest of scholars who have
documented a specific interdependence(Mowinkel, A. Bentzen, Kraeling,
Hooker). Yet Emerton has sought to emphasize the Hebrew origin of the Danielic vision and its imagery. "Such theories can be satisfactory only if
they pay adequate attention to the many points of contact between the Son
of Man sources and earlier Israelite tradition."[26] Regarding the origins
of the Similitudes of Enoch, the concept of the Anthropos in Iranian cul-
ture has been cited as an integral source(Bousset, Reitzenstein). Here too
Muilenburg warns against attributing too much significance to the possibility of such dependence. "I confess that my judgment has been influenc-
ed in part by the negative verdict of Duchesne-Guillemin. He not only rejects the equation of son of man and Iranian anthropos, but feels that Per-
sian influence upon apocalyptic has been exaggerated."[27]

As for IV Ezra it is widely held that it was written originally in
Hebrew by an author who was very much at home in the traditional surround-
ings of first century Judaism. Portions of the work are clearly reminiscent of the scene in Dan. 7. According to Box the incongruities between
the vision of the Man who arises from the sea and the interpretation giv-
en to it have resulted "from the author's own attempt to construct a vision out of mythological material which he did not fully comprehend but
wished to employ."[28] Both the Similitudes of Enoch and IV Ezra contain
elements which appear to be elaborations of the vision which is first
reported in Dan. 7.

All three works contain common features and themes. 1) The setting is
in heaven. Yet since the end of time has dawned, the spheres of heaven and
earth have been united. The actual setting is the new order of heaven and
earth at the beginning of the new aeon. It is this new order which empow-
ers the Man of IV Ezra to arise from the waves of the sea, fly with the
clouds, and stand on Mt. Zion just as in Dan. 7 beasts arise from the sea

The Apocalyptic View of the World

and thrones are placed in heaven. 2) The acts and deeds of the seers themselves during the last days are described along with all manner of signs and events which occur and will occur in that time. The new aeon has begun, but the order of events is proleptic since the seer describes the events which take place as he gazes into the future. In the Danielic vision the fourth beast and its counterpart encroach upon the Saints of the Most High and appear to threaten their immortality. In IV Ezra women give birth to monsters and bear children at three or four months of pregnancy. Enoch flies from high mountains on earth far into the reaches of heaven to gather up the secrets of wisdom during the last days.

3) A record of all earthly events and the secrets of heavenly wisdom reside in the omniscient mind of the Ancient of Days or the Most High who speaks to the seers in the vision. Only in the Similitudes of Enoch is "that Son of Man" who is also later named "that Son of a Woman" presented as a heavenly being who has pre-existed with the pre-existent God Most High from the beginning of time(I Enoch 48 and 62). 4) This heavenly one who has taken on human form and appearance is glorified and exalted, and set upon the throne of the God Most High to execute judgment upon the unrighteous. 5) The suffering of the transcendent, heavenly Redeemer and Judge and the heavenly hosts of the righteous is not a characteristic element of these apocalyptic works. Only in IV Ezra does suffering appear to be a possibility. Yet here as in I Enoch it is only the righteous on earth who perhaps suffer, not the transcendent Redeemer and the heavenly hosts. Ezra does report the death of the Messiah but this is not linked with suffering. There is no apparent connection between the Messiah and the Man who flies from the waves of the sea to the clouds with regard to their suffering. It is the seer Ezra alone, however, who makes the complaint that the existing earthly order continues too long.

6) It is of utmost importance that the transcendent Redeemer display

Johannine Language and Apocalyptic Vision

human characteristics in spite of the fact that this figure remains a heavenly being and never abides on earth. Only because he has taken on human form, can he be named as the one who judges. It is for this reason that the seer alludes to some sort of earthly birth or mentions a brief sojourn to the earthly realm. 7) The actual naming of Enoch himself as the Son of Man in I Enoch 70 is a baffling turn of events. Hooker finds a parallel here to Dan. 8,17 where Daniel is also addressed as son of man. She suggests that this is a logical development from the passage in Daniel since just as "the one like a son of man" is identified as an individual, so also Enoch himself who "walked with God" is viewed as a worthy candidate. Considering Dan. 8,17 Hooker makes the following, interesting query: "... is it possible that the author of the Similitudes, reading that passage, understood Daniel, the narrator of the vision, to be revealed here as himself the one like a Son of man whom he had seen in his previous vision?"[29] 8) Although the seer does not venture to give the precise future time of the end of the world(from Abraham to Abraham etc.), he strongly implies that the end is very near.

B The Synoptic Logia

Perhaps the greatest obstacle to the theory that Jesus derived his notion of the Son of Man from Dan. 7 is the fact that there is no evidence in that passage to support the concept of a suffering, apocalyptic Son of Man. Well over a third of the Synoptic sayings deal with this theme which is itself a central feature of the New Testament presentation of the messianic function. Whatever the source of the concept of the suffering Messiah might be, the suffering Servant of Second Isaiah, the suffering Royal Man or King, or the suffering Prophet, there is little doubt that the concept cannot have been developed on the basis of the Danielic heavenly Man,

The Synoptic Logia

I Enoch's glorified and exalted Son of Man, and IV Ezra's glorious Man who arises from the sea to judge the world from Mt. Zion.

For Borsch this is no cause for concern since he understands the New Testament Son of Man to be another manifestation of the Near Eastern Primal Man. In the legends of the First Man or King and the Primordial Man which he asserts are "inevitably bound one with another,"[30] he finds evidence for a pronounced, suffering motif which continues to influence the progressing myth. Yet with regard to the Son of Man concept in Jewish apocalyptic, he is definitely certain about the absence of this motif: "We notice that no suffering is explicitly predicated of this figure."[31] And commenting on the possible relationship between the Son of Man found in I Enoch and Second Isaiah's Servant he remarks: "What is more, and what is more to our point, to the extent that this Son of Man is related to the figure in II Isaiah, he is so in terms which do not involve a suffering Servant."[32]

Hooker finds support for a suffering Son of Man in Dan. 7 based on the supposed corporate nature of the figure who is depicted there. As the Saints of the Most High suffer, so also she presumes that the Son of Man suffers. A similar interdependence might be postulated between the Enochian Redeemer and the righteous on earth. It is reported that the cries of the righteous ascend to the Lord of the Spirits. Yet neither in Daniel or in I Enoch is it explicitly stated that "that Son of Man" or the "one like a son of man" suffers.

A striking feature of the earthly Son of Man sayings is the complete absence of apocalyptic imagery. The Son of Man of the present sayings never flies with the clouds of heaven. He is never depicted as having royal or heavenly attributes, nor is he ever exalted or glorified in a celestial sphere. It is true, however, that he often finds his life and mission on earth somewhat incongruous with the human mode of life in its earthly

Johannine Language and Apocalyptic Vision

sphere. Perhaps the dominant image here is that of the alienated traveler journeying through a foreign land. The earthly Synoptic Son of Man is not a pre-existent, supernaturally transcendent being. He does not ascend to the heavens to gather the secrets of wisdom from the heavenly court. The closest parallel to his essential nature is the image of the prophet. In this regard the comparison made between Jonah and the Son of Man is decisive. Not only is the Son of Man wise, humble, and alienated, attributes which fit most any prophet, he is also considered to be the only "sign" which is to be given to "this generation." Mt. 12,40: "For as Jonah was three days and three nights in the belly of the whale, so will the Son of Man be three days and nights in the heart of the earth." Mk. 10,45 is also related to the prophetic ideal: "For the Son of Man also came not to be served but to serve, and to give his life as a ransom for many."

The future sayings, however, present an entirely different Synoptic Son of Man figure. This is undoubtedly the Danielic heavenly Man. He flies on the clouds of heaven, appears at the end of time, and is invested with all heavenly power, glory, and authority, presumably to judge all of the nations of the earth. Mk. 13,26: "And they will see the Son of Man coming in clouds with great power and glory." Lk. 21,27: "And they will see the Son of Man coming in a cloud with power and great glory."

It is remarkable that Borsch claims to have found "no explicit quotations"[33] from the Danielic vision and sees this image of the Son of Man as a progression of the theme of the glorification and exaltation of the Primal Man and King. According to these sayings the Son of Man is to come "in clouds" or "in a cloud" and also "with power and glory." This wording is graphically representative of the event which is depicted in Dan. 7,13-14.

The exact setting of the Synoptic scene is a different matter. Many of the future, Synoptic logia suggest that the Son of Man will be viewed high in the heavens as he proceeds to earth for the judgment. Included in

The Synoptic Logia

this group are Mk. 13,26, Lk. 21,27, Mk. 8,38 and Mt. 24,30. Other sayings which can also be related to this motif, particularly to the concept of judgment on earth, are Mt. 10,23, Mt. 24, 27, Mt. 24,44, Mt. 16,28, Lk. 17,24, Lk. 17,22 and Lk. 12,40. The primary image operative here is that the Son of Man will come to earth at the end of time, and that the last judgment will occur when he holds court in the earthly realm. It should be observed that there is no mention of a celestial throne in these passages. The emphasis is on the "day of the Son of Man" on earth.

Other logia indicate that the setting referred to is the heavenly court. In these sayings the Son of Man is viewed as he is gloriously enthroned on the throne of God. As a consequence of his exaltation and the enthronement, the judgment of the peoples of the earth can commence from the heavenly sphere. This is the scene which is depicted in Mt. 19,28, Mt. 25,31, Lk. 22,69 and Lk. 12,8. An explicit parallel to the vision in Dan. 7 cannot be documented here. It is not said of the Son of Man in Daniel that he is seated and exalted on the throne of the Ancient of Days or that the authority to exercise judgment at the last judgment has been delegated to him alone. "And to him was given dominion and glory and kingdom, that all peoples, nations, and languages should serve him. ... But the Saints of the Most High shall receive the kingdom ... and judgment was given for the Saints of the Most High." The image of the Son of Man exalted and seated upon the throne of the Most High as the one who has been designated by God to judge the unrighteous is clearly reminiscent of the scene which is depicted in I Enoch 62.

Mt. 26,64 and Mk. 14,62 have been composed of images which represent both the enthronement motif in heaven and Jesus' journey to earth on the clouds of heaven at the day of judgment. Because these two themes are so very different and have been joined in such a blatant fashion, it is very likely that these are not authentic sayings. The two themes have been conflated in the obvious attempt to combine the theme of the authority of the Son of Man as the judge of the heavenly court with the expectation of the coming of Jesus to earth at the end of time. There is no evidence of a transitional portion of the saying which might have served to harmonize the two views. A likely explanation of this conflation is suggested by the context in which the two sayings are found. Both occur at that juncture in Mark and Matthew where Jesus is brought before the high priest Caiaphas. When Jesus is asked by Caiaphas if he actually professes to be the Christ, he responds with this saying. Both Mark and Matthew have intended the saying to be the utmost expression of Jesus' authority.

There is, therefore, no substantial support for the theory that the Synoptic Son of Man concept has been explicitly patterned on the actual figure of the transcendent redeemer and judge which is presented in the Jewish apocalyptic literature. There is much evidence which points to the verification of the theory proposed by Lindars, Leivestad, Colpe and others that a single, unified, consistent Son of Man concept based on the figure depicted in the works of Jewish apocalyptic never existed. There is also little indication that the concepts of the earthly Son of Man and the apocalyptic figure found in the Synoptic picture have been derived from a common source. All of the passion sayings of the Synoptic logia must be viewed as formations of the early church, if it is to be maintained that the use of the title in this regard is dependent upon the apocalyptic figure. The present sayings of the earthly Son of Man display no affinity for the apocalyptic figure and his transcendent nature. This leaves only the future sayings which must certainly have their origins in the apocalyptic milieu but which present such a confused rendering of apocalyptic themes and imagery that it appears highly unlikely that many of them, if any, can have been uttered by Jesus in a historical setting. It is not too far-fetched to suggest that the Synoptic Evangelists possessed merely an oral report

Three Johannine Sayings

that Jesus claimed to be the Son of Man, assumed that he had made reference to the apocalyptic figure, and then set out to validate that claim by extracting phrases from Daniel and I Enoch which they considered to be appropriate. Jesus' claim to the title, however, can nonetheless be considered to be an authentic claim.

C   Three Johannine Sayings

1) John 5,26-27: "For as the Father has life in himself, so he has granted the Son also to have life in himself, and has given him authority to execute judgment, because he is the Son of Man."

Stephen Smalley has rightly observed that the Synoptic division of the Son of Man sayings into three groups does not work for the Johannine sayings, since "there is a significant theological overlap between the groups."[34] Commenting on the fact that the Fourth Evangelist's christological perspective is more "rounded" and his eschatological perspective more "realized" than that of the Synoptists, Smalley adds: "It does not mean ... that the Johannine sayings cannot be in any sense original; and it need not mean that even the realized eschatology of these sayings must be completely detached from the underlying tradition on which(it is submitted) John was drawing independently."[35] Such a remark is in line with the prevailing consensus of opinion which ascribes the uniqueness of the Johannine perspective to the laspe of time between the setting for the Synoptic logia in the primitive community and that of the Johannine sayings as well as the influence of the development of a significantly different sociolgy(Martyn, Meeks). It has been postulated that the Fourth Evangelist greatly benefited from the early experience of the Synoptic communities and that he lived at precisely that point in time and history

Johannine Language and Apocalyptic Vision

which enabled him to reformulate the Christian κήρυγμα in a more sober, objective, and realistic mode of expression.

Surely the validity of this characterization of the Johannine sayings cannot be denied. All of them have been carefully crafted to reflect that particular insight attributed to the title, Son of Man, which can only be found in the Gospel of John. From a literary point of view 5,27 cannot be rated high on the list since it lacks the unique imagery that marks most of the other Johannine Son of Man sayings. Yet with regard to its theological content and particularly in view of its assumed relationship with the apocalyptic pronouncement found in Dan. 7, it is by far the most significant saying. J. Louis Martyn makes the following assertion in his assessment of the passage: "In some respects John 5,27 appears to be the most 'traditional' Son of Man saying in the whole of the New Testament."[36]

This saying identifies both the Father and the Son as the source of all life(as the Father has life so he has granted the Son life), and announces that the Father has therefore given the Son "authority to execute judgment, because he is the Son of Man." The saying is found in the second portion of a monologue uttered by Jesus in response to the controversy which arose between him and "the Jews" as a result of the healing which he performed on the Sabbath. In defense of the action the Evangelist reports that Jesus first answered: "My Father is working still and I am working," a statement which reportedly the Jews interpreted to be the verification of Jesus' claim to be equal with God. The ensuing monologue takes up this theme and seeks to elucidate the working relationship between Jesus and the Father.

Dodd and Gaechter have convincingly arguered that a parable related to "a series of references from the Oxyrhynchus papyri(from Egypt of NT times)"[37] stands behind vv. 19-20a. These verses certainly echo a familiar theme of Johannine theologizing(7,28; 8,42; 3,34; 8,26; 12,49), yet

John 5,27

it is evident that an axiomatic action is being referred to here. Brown and Lindars accept the role of the parable as a basis for the discourse, the setting of which could be "in an apprentice shop where a youth is learning a trade."[38] The format of the parable which consists of three axiomatic statements precisely parallels vv. 19-20a. Brown, Lindars, and Gaechter consider v. 30 to be a displaced portion of the parable.

According to Brown the Johannine tradition preserves two separate forms of the discourse of which vv. 21-25 form one unit and vv. 26-29 the second. Each section is based on the same themes of giving life and judging. VV. 21-25 clearly present these themes in terms of the Johannine concept of realized eschatology which Brown relates to the work of healing on the Sabbath. VV 26-29 take up the same themes in accordance with the dictates of final eschatology. Bultmann holds that this division can be attributed to the role of the ecclesiastical redactor who has inserted not only the apocalyptic title in v. 27 but who has also added vv. 28-29, "trying to conform John's realized eschatology to the official eschatology of the Church."[39] Boismard considers vv. 26-30 to be the earlier form of the discourse, since its eschatological outlook resembles that found in the Synoptics. Vanhoye argues that the entire passage "is a whole and must be interpreted as such."[40] With regard to Bultmann's division of the passage according to two different concepts of eschatology, Brown insists that "such a dichotomy between the two eschatologies is unwarranted."[41]

Certainly Bultmann shows a great lack of perception of the Evangelist's careful and masterful presentation of the term Son of Man when he claims that v. 27 is an unnecessary and clumsy repetition. Moloney is most correct to point out that the phrase is "not without importance"[42] in that section of the discourse which is bound by vv. 19-30. It is generally agreed that the appearance of the accepted apocalyptic title in the second section of the discourse, vv. 26-30, serves to accommodate the

Johannine Language and Apocalyptic Vision

the Johannine program of "realized eschatology" to the traditional apocalyptic expectation which is operative in the Synoptics. It has been assumed that Dan. 7 is the most likely source of the term, and that since John has seen fit to include it here, he is directly alluding to the transcendent, heavenly Redeemer of Jewish apocalyptic.

It is certain, however, that the unique and special imagery employed by the author of Daniel to introduce this figure is totally lacking here. The setting is an earthly scene in the life of Jesus rather than the heavenly court. No mention is made of the Son of Man flying "in," "on," or "with" the clouds of heaven. There is also no allusion to a future audience of Jesus as the Son of Man before the court of his Father or the Ancient of Days, which is sometimes indicated by the Synoptic logia. There is, therefore, no clear indication that this scene in John parallels the enthronement scene found in I Enoch where the Son of Man is glorified and exalted before the heavenly hosts. Neverhteless, this scene is decidedly that of the last judgment. V. 21 mentions the role of the Father in raising the dead, and vv. 25, 28, and 29 point to the hour when the spiritually dead and the physically dead will hear the voice of the Son. Although vv. 28-29 appear to reflect the saying which is found in Dan. 12,2, there is no definite reference here to an apocalyptic depiction of the last judgment.

Both Moloney and Martyn are convinced that the wording of v. 27 and the anarthrous use of the term precisely reflect Dan. 7,13-14, particularly with regard to the rendering of this verse in the LXX. The word, "dominion," in Dan. 7 is rendered by ἐξουσίαν both in the LXX and in John. Yet a closer look at Dan. 7 indicates that it is not at all certain that that passage serves to verify the titular usage of the term. Both Dan. 7 and Theodotian Daniel use the expression, "one like a son of man." Here it is obviously the indefinite <u>bar nash</u> which serves as the basis for the phrase. This increases the likelihood for ambiguity and clearly points to the generic usage. Nevertheless, it would be nonsensical to translate the term to mean "humankind" or "man," and to understand it in a predicative sense as the object of the sentence or to view it as the predicate nominative of the clause.

This line of reasoning points to a crucial aspect of the term which has not often been considered. Although many scholars have posited a non-Israelite origin for the concept of the figure of the transcendent Redeemer, it is highly likely that the theological and philological source for Daniel's expression, "one like a son of man," lies in the Hebrew scriptures themselves. The phrase is very clearly reminiscent of the poetic usages of ben adam in the Psalms, where it is used singularly and also in a parallel construction with adam. In these passages the Psalmist apparently uses the term in a generic sense to refer to humankind as "son of man," "sons of men," or those like the "sons of men." It is not clear, however, that the function of the term in these passages is limited to this role. Dodd's study of Ps. 80 has isolated the corporate sense of the phrase based on its use as the designation of one who is representative of humankind as a whole. Obviously, this usage is related to the occurrence of the term in Ezekiel and Daniel as a form of address; it appears to be used here as a prophetic designation. The Semitic character of the term has long been recognized.

Moloney finds definite evidence that the Evangelist has employed the term for reasons other than the function related to its assumed apocalyptic background. As the discourse indicates, Father and Son are uniquely bound together. V. 21 emphasizes the fact that even as the Father raises the dead and gives life, so also the Son carries out the same functions. The same is true with regard to the act of judgment. Yet v. 22 announces that the Father judges no one and that he has given all judgment to the

Johannine Language and Apocalyptic Vision

Son. Continuing this progression of thought in relation to v. 27, Moloney rightly points out "that not only does the Son have all judgment, given to him by the Father, but that he also exercises this judgment (κρίσιν ποιεῖν), because he is the Son of Man."[43] Jesus as the Son of Man on earth is the place where revelation and judgment occur, both in the present and the future. Moloney thus finds the title to be used almost in a passive sense as a "locus revelationis." The Evangelist has specifically stated that the Son came not to judge the world and that neither does the Father judge. It is very clear, however, that by virtue of the unique fact of the incarnation, the presense of the Son precipitates the judgment.

Seen from this perspective the term Son of Man functions as an integral part of the entire discourse which includes vv. 19-30, and is not dependent upon its presumed apocalyptic function for its role in the monologue. It is in fact nothing more than a precise determination of the relation between the Father and the Son with regard to the judgment which accompanies the incarnation. It is used to determine and describe the judging role given to the Son in v. 22. As Brown asserts, there is no great gulf between the "realized eschatology" of vv. 19-25 and the final eschatology of vv. 26-30. Without vv. 28-29 there is absolutely no indication that the Evangelist has the day of final judgment in view. Yet this relationship follows logically from the traditional, eschatological expectation of the Evangelist and reflects the words of Jesus. It does not arise out of an apocalyptic view of the last judgment.

Schnackenburg is not certain that vv. 28-29 have been derived from Dan. 12,2 or that these verses point to a definite doctrine of the resurrection of the dead, although he is confident that such an expectation was prevalent in primitive Christianity. It is nonetheless significant that he finds that these verses have a negligible impact on the passage. Even though he considers them to be traditional, apocalyptic elements

John 5,27

which have been inserted at a later redaction, he does not find them incongruous to the essential, "realized," eschatological thrust of the passage.[44]

Martyn has convincingly shown that the identification of Jesus as the Mosaic-Prophet-Messiah was considered to be a legitimate phase in the growth of faith in the Johannine community. Proceeding by means of his own, unique, anti-midrashic midrash, the Evangelist demonstrates that a complete understanding of Jesus is bound up in his identity as the Son of Man on earth. This is indeed a remarkable discovery which provides support for the theory that the term Son of Man was originally a prophetic designation(Ezekiel), since the essential nature of Jesus as the Son of Man is thus found to be directly related to his prophetic role as the Mosaic Prophet.

It is well-known that the Fourth Evangelist will hear nothing of a Davidic Messiah. Although the typical pattern documented by Martyn cannot be isolated in this passage, chapter 5 itself does end in a midrashic discussion which is concerned with Moses. An element common to the four passages identified by Martyn is present here also. Jesus declares that the understanding of his identity is not midrashic, i.e. the Jews search the scriptures for eternal life and do not perceive the witness which they hear from Jesus.(v. 39) Not only do the people not believe Jesus, Jesus can, therefore, accuse them of not believing Moses, for it was Moses who "wrote" of him in the scriptures.(v. 46) In this manner Jesus turns the tables on the midrashic method of the Jews and asserts that it is Moses himself who accuses them because they have not accepted his teaching.

Could it not be that just as a facsimile of Martyn's midrashic dialogue has been reversed at the end of this chapter, so also the identification of Jesus as the Son of Man is to be understood not according to the dictates of the apocalyptic view of the last judgment but rather in

Johannine Language and Apocalyptic Vision

terms of the qualities ascribed to the Mosaic-Prophet-Messiah? It is highly probable that John 5,27 is an authentic saying of Jesus. Certainly it is a traditional saying which lays the foundation of Jesus' claim to be the Son of Man. Yet it is not at all clear that it points to Dan. 7. It appears rather to indicate that Jesus himself vigorously rejected the apocalyptic figure whom Daniel identified as the Son of Man and acknowledged only a figure which has its origin in the prophetic tradition. Jesus, the Incarnate Son, is also the eschatological Judge of all peoples and ages present and future because he too is "one like a prophet."

2) John 6,62: "Then what if you were to see the Son of Man ascending where he was before?"

This is indeed one of the strangest Son of Man sayings in all of the New Testament. The immediate response which it calls forth from the reader is that he posit a permanent place in heaven for the Son of Man which has endured from the beginning of time presumably until Jesus' appearance on earth. This in turn leads the reader to the assumption that although people in Jesus' day might "see" him ascend to heaven, the present age and the earthly state of the world would continue unchanged, even though the Son of Man would be glorified by his return to the heavenly court. Such an understanding follows as a necessary consequence of the statement, since the proof of Jesus' identity as the Son of Man is to result from the witness of those who remain on earth in its regular state peering into heaven at the Son of Man "where he was before." In other words, people on earth should have "seen" him in heaven even before he came to earth. The course of events to which the saying alludes is undoubtedly alien to the function of the apocalyptic Son of Man and the traditional, apocalyptic view of the end of time. Jesus' comment can thus be seen to be a sa-

John 6,62

tirical play on words directed against traditional, apocalyptic expectations.

Traditionally, the saying has been held to be an incomplete clause, the meaning of which is not clear. It is an aposiopesis, a conditional clause which has a protasis but which lacks an apodosis.[45] Several apodoses have been proposed based on a presumed reaction to the following statements: a) the scandal mentioned in v. 61; b) Jesus' claim to be the bread of life which has come down from heaven which is found in vv. 48-50; c) the Eucharistic references to the Son of Man in vv. 51-58.[46] The apodoses proposed by Bultmann and Bauer presuppose that the scandal in v. 61 is related to the whole of the preceeding Bread of Life Discourse and its emphasis on the Eucharist. Bultmann develops the a fortiori argument: "Clearly we have to understand: 'Then the offence really will be great!'" Bauer, on the other hand, suggests that Jesus intends to solve the riddle of his teaching on the feeding of the multitude by proving that he had not required anthropophagy: "If the condition is fulfilled (the people will see him ascend to heaven), the offence will be diminished or removed."[47] According to Westcott it is the event at Calvary which combines both the negative and positive reactions to the protasis, since it seems clear that the ascension which is referred to here is that of the resurrection of Jesus. "The offence must be faced and the costly decision made before man can eat and drink the flesh and blood of Christ and, being united with him in death, receive the gift of eternal life."[48]

Brown holds the view that the title, the Son of Man, refers to the figure which both Daniel and I Enoch characterize as celestial. Moloney and Borsch contend that the concept of pre-existence is a primary feature of the saying. Considering the possibility that the saying is the work of the Evangelist, Borsch proposes a variety of likely sources for the logion which include themes related to 6,27, 6,53 and 3,13. He concludes that it

Johannine Language and Apocalyptic Vision

is an authentic saying or fragment other than the Johannine Son of Man saying found in 3,13 but one which has been derived from the same matrix of ideas and themes.[49] Brown also calls to mind the parallel to Jesus' conversation with Nicodemus and, pointing to v. 63, asserts that it is only the ascended Son of Man who can give the Spirit.[50] Moloney proposes that the Evangelist is using the concept of the pre-existent Son of Man to counter the old controversy and polemic also related to 3,13 that the great patriarchs, prophets, and especially Moses had ascended on high to receive the revelation of God.[51]

Brown agrees that Bornkamm has conclusively shown that vv. 60-71 do do not refer to vv. 51-58, the Eucharistic homily, but rather to the themes which are found in vv. 35-50. He points out "that all the references in 60-71 concern hearing or believing Jesus' doctrine; there is not a single reference to refusing to eat his flesh or drink his blood."[52] For Brown the crucial verse of this section is v. 63; he contends that the contrast between Spirit and flesh in this verse parallels that found in 3,6. "Jesus is not speaking of eucharistic flesh but of flesh as he spoke of it in ch. iii, namely, the natural principle in man which cannot give eternal life."[53] Therefore, the reference to Spirit here has nothing "to do with a spiritual interpretation of the presence of Jesus in the Eucharist."[54]

Moloney agrees with this interpretation but claims to have shown "that vv. 51-58 are not to be regarded as uniquely Eucharistic or secondary but as a continuation of basic Johannine christological themes found in vv. 35-50."[55] It is his opinion that v. 62 does not refer to the ascension of Jesus but that it is in fact only a rhetorical question which serves to highlight Jesus' claim to be the Son of Man, the unique revealer, by focusing on Jesus the pre-existent Logos who has been revealed as the Son of Man. If v. 62 were a clear reference to the ascen-

John 6,62

sion, he contends that it would very likely have contained the use of the verb, ὑψωθῆναι. Yet even so it would be a clumsy sentence, since "where he was before" is in his view not a reference to the ascension motif but rather "to some sort of pre-existence."[56]

Proceeding from this framework Moloney asserts that there is no need for Jesus, the pre-existent 'Logos' and eternal Son, to ascend. "To ask that he ascend is completely to misunderstand his origin."[57] V. 63 then becomes a typical Johannine answer to v. 62. It is essentially an accusation in which Jesus accuses the disciples and the other listeners of seeking only after the things of the "flesh." Here Moloney interprets "flesh" as Brown does, but adds: "It is certainly not a contradiction of vv. 51-58."[58] Thus v. 62 can be viewed as a rhetorical question which is used to counter the offences generated by the entire discourse by pointing out the following assertion: "There is only one life-giving principle: the the word of Jesus, i.e., the revelation of God which is to be found in the Son of Man."[59]

Borsch points up the similarity between the final clause of v. 62, "where he was before," and the addition to 3,13, "who is in heaven," which is preserved by a number of manuscripts. If the term Son of Man is an actual prophetic designation which also served as a means of address, then these two clauses highlight its paradoxical nature. Ezekiel is not addressed as Son of Man because of his human birth or by virtue of his own achievements. On the contrary, he is honored by the address precisely because he has responded to the Word of the Lord in spite of his human condition and limitations. It is only the echo and reflection of the divine call within him which enables him to respond to the divine presence.

This is precisely what Jesus demands of the disciples and the remnant of the multitude which remains before him. As the pre-existent Logos and the eternal Son, he is co-eternal with the Father. He shares

Johannine Language and Apocalyptic Vision

the divine presence with the Father, that very presence to which all of the prophets responded. The prophetic designation itself, therefore, serves only as a means of acknowledging the presence on high which has manifested itself in the human sphere on earth. As the Incarnate Son, however, Jesus is the Son of Man, the one who was pre-existent with the Father destined to be revealed to all peoples of the earth. It is this fact which the rhetorical question seeks to elucidate. Moses, the patriarchs, and all of the prophets responded to his presence. In an essential, qualitative way of viewing the matter, one could say that they "saw" him in heaven from their vantage point on earth.

Yet by virtue of the incarnation this same Son of Man has actually appeared in the flesh on earth. By demanding that the disciples and the remnant of the multitude become aware of the Spirit which gives life, Jesus is simply asking that they acknowledge the phenomenal relationship which exists between the true, heavenly Son of Man and the very one who has appeared before them. He asks only that they "see" him "where he was before." Then they would understand why his words about eating and drinking the flesh and blood of the Son of Man are not scandalous. It is only from an uncanny, ironical, retrospective, and secondary frame of reference which looks out over the span of Christ's life and encompasses the sadness and glory of it all that the saying refers to Jesus' passion, death, and resurrection.

3) John 9,35: "Jesus heard that they had cast him out, and having found him he said, 'Do you believe in the Son of Man?'"

This saying is significantly located at the end of chapter 9 which is a remarkable display of the Evangelist's dramatic skill. The story of the healing of the man born blind is told with a great appreciation for

John 9,35

the intrigue and suspense it must have generated among the participants and listeners alike, and the theological import of the incident is laid out with an amazing candor. Jesus' question directed to the blind man is in itself very remarkable. Not only does it add one last dramatic element of surprise to the story at a moment when it seems that the Evangelist's aims have already been accomplished, it is unprecedented as a Son of Man logion. Nowhere else in the New Testament is the verb, πιστεύω, used with reference to the title, and no other recorded episode indicates Jesus' eagerness to identify himself in such a direct manner as the Son of Man. Martyn sums up the uniqueness of the saying by asserting: "Nowhere else in gospel tradition does the Jesus who walks among men on the face of the earth require of someone the confession of himself as the Son of Man."[60]

Bultmann places chapter 9 at the beginning of the section which he entitles, "The Light of the World." It is comprised of selected sections from chapters 8, 12, and 10. Moloney disagrees that this rearrangement is necessary. He points out that chapter 8 is constructed around the claim of Jesus to be the light of the world and finds the theme of chapter 10, Jesus' proclamation that he is the Good Shepherd, to be a harmonizing theme. In addition he calls attention to the bitter polemic between Jesus and the Pharisees which has been recorded in chapters 8-10.[61] Actually, this debate begins in chapter 7. It is also important to note that the healing of the blind man by means of the spittle and the water from the pool of Siloam can be related to the water ceremonies of the Feast of Tabernacles which is announced at the beginning of chapter 7. As Brown indicates, "it was the water from this same pool of Siloam that was used in the ceremony at Tabernacles."[62]

According to Martyn the blind man's confession of Jesus as the Son of Man is the last step in a midrashic sequence in which the Evangelist

Johannine Language and Apocalyptic Vision

develops an account of the debate between the Johannine Church and the Synogogue, centered on the progression of the belief in Jesus as the Mosaic-Prophet-Messiah to a more mature faith of him as the Son of Man. When one considers the fact that this debate begins in chapter 7, it becomes evident that this motif is a central feature of chapters 7, 8, 9, and 10.

The debate concerns the confusion which arose from a number of conflicting, messianic expectations which were prevalent in Jesus' day. As Martyn indicates, it appears that the controversy has been narrowed in scope in chapter 9. Both the Johannine Church and the Pharisees agree that the Mosaic-Prophet-Messiah must perform miracles. The Pharisees disagree, however, that Jesus has worked a genuine miracle and claim that he cannot be the prophet promised by Moses.[63] Cullmann thinks that 9,35 indicates that John like Paul was familiar with the ανθρωπος or Son of Man concept as a "fundamental christological interpretation"[64] prominent in a Jewish-Christian environment. Borsch thinks that this section of chapter 9 has been heavily reworked to remove evidence of a time when the Son of Man played a much more vital role in the tradition.[65]

The themes of light and judgment flow together here as the result of the blind man's confession. Moloney notes the parallel to Mark 8 where the cure of a blind man is followed by a discussion of the blindness of the disciples but "preceeds the Petrine confession(8,29) which Jesus corrects in terms of 'the Son of Man' (8,31)."[66] Also the possible significance of Isaiah 6,9 cannot be overlooked here. Brown suggests that there is much support for the argument that the Evangelist's account of the healing of the blind man was intended for baptismal use. In vv. 38-39 he uncovers an addition which has obviously been taken from a non-Johannine source related to baptismal liturgy and catechesis. Not only does the nature of the miracle call forth the baptismal motif, the act of giving

45

John 9,35

sight is related to the theme of "enlightenment" which "was a term used of NT authors to refer to Baptism."[67] He does not, however, find support for the theory that John 9,35 was a confessional, baptismal formulation used by the Johannine Church, although there is much evidence that it was used by the early church as an integral part of the ceremony held on "the day of great scrutiny" for those catechumens deemed worthy of Baptism.

Barrett holds the view that this unique logion is due to the concept of the heavenly Man which lies behind the Son of Man title. He contends that both John and the blind man are aware that Jesus' question points to such a figure, one who is "the sole means of union between heaven and earth."[68] Thus the blind man knowingly asks that this one be indicated to him. Moloney finds that the more traditional, apocalyptic concept is evident here and asserts that the saying shows the force of John's concept of realized eschatology carried to its most logical extreme. The debate with the Pharisees revolves around the fact that they do not recognize Jesus' origin. They do not know "from where he is" (πόθεν ἐστίν v. 29) as the blind man does. Moloney points to Dodd's emphasis of Jesus' statement that he is "ἐκ τῶν ἄνω." It is by virtue of this unique origin that Jesus makes his claim to be the supreme revealer who has been given the authority to judge in a true and consequential, eschatological manner.

Yet there is a unique twist to this understanding which Moloney finds characteristic of John. As the Son of Man Jesus is the place of revelation, the light of the world, and the eschatological judge. It is not he himself, however, who initiates judgment. Since he is the very manifestation(incarnation) of God's revelation to the world, he is the place where people judge themselves. In stark contrast to this view is that of Ragnar Leivestad who asserts that the term Son of Man in John 9, 35 is not used messianically at all. It is his opinion that if it were

Johannine Language and Apocalyptic Vision

intended to be a messianic title, the blind man would simply have answered "Yes" or "No."[69] Brown notes that the blind man's query is a "curious question," "since the man already knows that Jesus is a prophet (17), has unique powers(32), and comes from God(33)."[70]

There can be no doubt that the confession of the blind man defies the traditional, apocalyptic world-view. Rather than being named in heaven before the heavenly court by the God Most High, Jesus is proclaimed to be the Son of Man in a mundane, earthly setting by a man whom he had never met prior to the event of the healing. His enthronement and glorification in the heavenly court do not follow as a result of this recognition, and the judgment of the world does not take place in the expected apocalyptic setting. As the discussion with the Pharisees continues to unfold, Jesus allows them to judge themselves.

Taking into account Leivestad's observation that the term is not used as a messianic designation here and Brown's comment about the blind man's question in light of the obvious lack of apocalyptic motifs in the chapter, it is rather unlikely that the Evangelist could have used the apocalyptic tradition as a source for the title. As Borsch points out the Evangelist passes up a sterling opportunity in v. 38 to allow the blind man to declare most emphatically, "Lord, I believe in the Son of Man!" In spite of his apparent eagerness to identify Jesus as the eschatological Redeemer, the Evangelist restrains his enthusiasm and proceeds very cautiously to accomplish his task. There is no conclusive proof that the blind man even understood the significance of the title (see 12,34). He appears to be solely dependent upon Jesus' knowledge not only for the naming of the person who is the Son of Man but also for an explanation of the very title itself. One can only speculate about the reason why the Evangelist chose not to be more forthcoming at this crucial juncture. It must be concluded, therefore, that the confes-

John 9,35

sion of the blind man points to a Son of Man tradition related to the messianic expectation of the Mosaic-Prophet-Messiah, yet clearly distinguished from it.

III The Prophet

A) John 6,53: "So Jesus said to them, 'Truly, truly, I say to you, unless you eat the flesh of the Son of Man and drink his blood, you have no life in you."

Nowhere else in the Gospel of John does one find the Mosaic typology and symbology more prominent than in the sixth chapter. Acknowledging in the story of the feeding of the multitude the Evangelist's aim to present Jesus as the Mosaic-Prophet-Messiah or the "new Moses," Borsch wishfully conjectures that "it may be that these are largely elaborations on a story of a rather different character,"[71] hoping thereby to establish a foothold on which to set his Royal Man. He makes a rather futile attempt to see the feeding of the multitude "as a kind of proleptic anticipation"[72] of a heavenly meal that was to take place in the future in order to salvage his theory of the Man feeding his people.

Yet even if one postulates that the kingly and also perhaps apocalyptic elements have been discarded, there is no evidence in the text which supports such a view. The presentation of Jesus as the Mosaic-Prophet-Messiah is a pronounced feature of the story, and there can be no doubt that the Bread of Life Discourse has been designed to clarify those false and inadequate, messianic expectations which came to the fore in response to the crowd's recognition of Jesus as the Prophet.

Following the account of the feeding of the five thousand, it is reported in v. 41 that "the people saw the sign which he had done" and proclaimed him to be "the prophet." Their subsequent attempt to make Jesus

John 6,53

a king marks a sharp division in the text. At this point in the account everyone is scattered, including the disciples. As Dodd indicates, it is the miracle of Jesus walking on the water and the solemn "I am" pronouncement which provides a new orientation for the original "sign" or miracle. This in turn helps to set the tone and provides for the general structure of the discourse which follows.[73] It is the Evangelist's purpose to present a proper interpretation of the feeding of the multitude and to estabish, thereby, a progression of the understanding of Jesus' messiahship from his identity as a new Moses-like figure to a more complete concept.

The structure of chapter 6, particularly that of the Bread of Life Discourse which is contained in vv. 25-65, is one of the most complex and baffling portions of the Gospel of John. It is not clear whether it has been intended as a sapiential discussion or a Eucharistic exposition or both. The primary debate concerns the determination of the essential nature of vv. 51-58. Since the Evangelist has not included in his Gospel a report of the institution of the Last Supper similar to the Synoptic accounts, it has been assumed that this homily is the Johannine equivalent. Yet there appears to be no means of determining with any degree of certainty whether or not these verses provide an actual account of the Eucharist.

Bultmann claims that vv. 51c-58 are clearly an addition which has come from the hands of the ecclesiastical redactor and that this section is fully Eucharistic. Not only has the title, the Son of Man, been added in v. 53 and v. 27, Bultmann also finds that the phrase, "I will raise him up at the last day," which has its original place in v. 54, has been added to vv. 39, 40, and 44.[74] Brown finds Eucharistic themes in the two sections of the body of the discourse, vv. 25-34 and vv. 35-50, as well as in the multiplication and the transitional verses, and asserts that the "chapter would be eucharistic if 51-58 were not a part of it."[75] Nevertheless, he postulates that vv. 51-58 had a different origin than the rest of the discourse and that the Eucharistic element present there is primary. His theory is that the section comprised of vv. 51-58 "is made up of material from the Johannine narrative of the institution of the Eucharist which was originally located in the Last Supper scene and that this material has been recast into a duplicate of the Bread of Life Discourse."[76] He is particularly impressed by 6,51 which he thinks resembles an institutional formula. He also holds the view that vv. 51-58 were probably not added to vv. 35-50 until the final stage of editing.

A number of scholars find that the emphasis of the entire Bread of Life Discourse is on the concept of the earthly Jesus who reveals God on earth. Jesus is "flesh and blood," perfect humanity, and it is his human life which provides the means by which God makes himself known to all peoples. Thus for Odeberg, for example, the realism of vv. 51-58 has nothing to do with the Eucharist. It is his opinion that this section refers emphatically to the reality of Jesus: "the acquisition of the heavenly bread, the 'imperishable food,' was no mere allegory."[77] On the opposite end of the spectrum are those who consider the whole discourse to be fully Eucharistic: "Cullmann finds Eucharistic references in almost every verse."[78] Some divide the discourse into two sections. "VV. 35-50(51) speak in purely sapiential terms about the revelation of God in and by Jesus, while vv. 51-58 refer to the Eucharistic flesh of Jesus."[79] Finally, there are those who discover both revelatory and Eucharistic themes and elements scattered throughout the entire discourse.

Peder Borgen sees the whole discourse as a single, unified tradition and claims to have uncovered the source and structure on which it has been based. It is actually a Jewish-Christian homily similar to the ones which he finds in Philo and the Rabbinic literature. Common to the lit-

John 6,53

erature of both of these sources was a tradition of the fathers of Israel eating manna in the desert. Examining the isolated homiletic structures, Borgen has "pointed out several midrashic features which are common parts of Philo, John and the Palestinian midrash: the systematic paraphrase of words from Old Testament quotations and fragments of some haggadic traditions, and the use of widespread homiletic pattern."[80] Many of these texts reflect Jewish, eschatological expectations concerning the Prophet-like-Moses who was to come on Passover accompanied by the appearance of manna.

Comparing Mut. 253-263, Leg. All. III, 162-168, and John 6, Borgen shows that John's use of haggadic tradition follows the same homiletic pattern. He also finds other common elements in the midrashic development of an Old Testament text. The homily often paraphrases the Old Testament quotation word by word and sometimes presupposes other verses. Besides the opening key text, there is also a secondary text. Philo's secondary text is taken from the Torah, while John has taken his text from one of the prophets(Jn. 6,45=Is. 54,13). While there is much Rabbinic evidence which shows that bread was thought of as an equivalent for Torah, it is noteworthy that in Mut. 259 Philo replaces the Old Testament ἄρτον with wisdom, τὴν σοφίαν, in much the same manner that John replaces the same word with τὴν σάρκα.[81]

Moloney is convinced that the discourse in its present form is a coherent unit and was used meaningfully by the early church. He asserts that the entire discourse is primarily sapiential and that its theme is set forth in vv. 29, 40, 47, 54, and 58: it is a belief in Jesus, the unique revealer of the Father, which leads to eternal life. Jesus is the bread of life of a wholly different order than manna was a heavenly food for the fathers of Israel. Moloney does not think that the Eucharistic homily is an addition and finds vv. 51-52 to be typically Johannine. The

homily is certainly proof of an Eucharistic celebration in the Johannine
Church, yet "John appears to be developing a very important, sapiential
line of thought, without interruption, from vv. 26-58. To do this he has
used current midrashic method, into which he has introduced language
which comes directly from the Eucharistic celebrations which he knew."[82]
Thus for Moloney the Eucharist plays a secondary but essential role which
shows the Evangelist's familiarity with the community practice of the
Eucharist and its relatedness to the sapiential theme which he has proclaimed throughout the discourse.

The importance of the parallels to the Wisdom Literature of the Old
Testament which are found in the discourse and their significance for the
Son of Man concept cannot be overlooked. It has been recognized that the
Johannine Son of Man functions in a manner often analogous to that of the
concept of wisdom. It has been suggested that John's ascending and de-
scending Son of Man has been patterned on wisdom personified, the figure
Sophia, who descends from heaven to search for an earthly habitation and
who usually ascends on high soon thereafter when no earthly abode is
found. In determining the primary, sapiential charcter of the body of the
discourse, vv. 35-50, Brown points to a host of parallels to the themes
of the Wisdom Literature. With regard to the theme mentioned in v. 31
which is grounded in Exod. 16,4 and 15 and also Num. 11 but which is related to Wis. 16,20 as well, Brown shows that Sir. 24,21, Prov. 9,5, and
Sir. 15,3 all reflect the symbology of the discourse.

The Jesus who is depicted here is very much like Wisdom of Prov. 9,
5: "Come, eat of my bread; drink of the wine I have mixed." The Wisdom
which is described in Sir. 15,3 promises nourishment and drink for the
one who fears God and practices the Torah: "She will nourish him with
the bread of understanding and give him the water of learning to drink."
The words of Amos 8,11-13 appear to have been derived from the same con-

cept, yet deal with a negative result.[83] In his claim that there is "nothing startlingly new" in vv. 35-50, Moloney sees Jesus' proclamation that he is the bread of life as a continuation of the theme which is found in v. 31. He also points to a number of parallels to the Wisdom Literature which include Sir. 14,9, Sir. 24,21, Wis. 16,20-26, and Is. 55,1-3. There can be no doubt about John's allusion to the messianic banquet described in Is. 65 and Is. 55. The Evangelist depicts Jesus as the source of messianic food who has come down from heaven and who invites everyone to the banquet. In Jesus the old Israelite prophecy has been fulfilled. The time of the banquet is now, since the eschatological end of time has been realized by the incarnation of the eternal Son. All of this is so because of the unique revelation which Jesus has brought. It is for this reason that he can proclaim to all who partake of his banquet that he "will raise (them) up at the last day."

The introduction to the discourse is dependent upon the typical Johannine technique of misunderstanding for its effect. Seeking to verify the authority of Jesus' teaching and his "sign," the crowd demands in vv. 31-33 that he give them manna as proof that he is indeed the "new Moses" according to the current, messianic expectations. Although they have proclaimed him to be "the prophet" because he fed them, still they are not certain that he is the "new Moses" since they have seen no evidence of manna. Reverting to the Jewish style of exegesis which Borgen has identified, Jesus corrects the Old Testament quotation from Exod. 16, 4 and redefines the role of Moses in giving the Israelites manna from heaven. He solemnly declares that it was not Moses who <u>gave</u> them the manna, but rather his Father who <u>gives</u> them the true bread from heaven.

By pointing out the essential, sapiential character of the entire discourse, Moloney consistently shows how the primary theme which is announced in v. 29 is operative throughout the discourse. With regard to

6,53 he can therefore demonstrate how it functions in its own environment in a manner similar to that of 6,27. "However, this revelation has its validity (see v. 55) from the fact that he has been sent by the Father (v. 57), that he has come down from heaven (v. 58). What is being claimed by Jesus here is a repetition of what has already been said in v. 27. Now the "food" is specified: it is the body and blood of the Son of Man."[84] Moloney then recalls the future tense of John 6,27 and points out its relevance. Although the Son of Man gives the true bread from heaven and is indeed that bread himself, his unique role as revealer is ultimately bound up with the spilling of his blood on the cross. Thus both 6,53 and 6,27 point beyond Jesus' homily to the final moment of revelation on the cross. The Son of Man, therefore, is the place where God is revealed. Jesus is not only a "new Moses;" he is in essence the crucified Son of Man.[85]

It has been stated above that the term Son of Man in the Gospel of John serves as both a prophetic designation and a messianic title, and that the Evangelist has used it interchangeably to refer Jesus' messianic role and his prophetic character. It is here in the sixth chapter that this fact can best be demonstrated. First of all there is absolutely no evidence that the term functions as an apocalyptic title in the discourse. The emphasis is on the present reality of Jesus' revelation and the eternal life which comes from the "food" which the Son of Man gives. (The present tense is widely attested here, although Brown thinks that the future tense is to be preferred.)[86] If one believes in Jesus and partakes of his food, then such a person will be raised up by Jesus "at the last day."

The discourse distinguishes sharply between the present and "the last day." Nonetheless, it emphasizes that God's ultimate revelation has been made manifest in the person Jesus. This view is evidence of the traditional, Jewish eschatological expectancy which is expounded in the pro-

John 6,53

phetic writings. There is no trace of apocalyptic imagery to be found throughout this entire chapter. There are no clouds or angels from heaven to symbolize the apocalyptic end of time. Jesus is the Son of Man who abides solemnly on earth and anticipates a day of judgment, even though that judgment has ultimately been manifested in his own person. He gives no indication that the great, prophetic day of judgment in a final, traditional, eschatological, and historical sense is imminent.

It is the fact of the incarnation which molds the discourse into a complete, harmonious unit. At first glance it appears that v. 27, v. 32, and v. 35 all contradict one another. The crowd is first told to labor for the food "which endures to eternal life," which only the Son of Man gives. Next Jesus rejects their demand for manna and resolutely proclaims that it is only the Father who "gives ... the true bread from heaven." And finally to the great astonishment of all assembled there, he declares that he himself is "the bread of life." All of these statements are true, and yet they are all dependent upon 6,53 for their final clarification.

As a prophetic designation the paradoxical term Son of Man referred conversely to the God who addressed the prophet. Since Ezekiel is addressed as "Son of Man," he acknowledges the God who has called on him, that unique God upon whom he is dependent for spiritual knowledge. There is a parallel to this concept in the discourse itself; and it is significant that it is a quotation from the secondary text which has been taken from the prophetic writings of the Old Testament rather than the Torah as is usually found in Philo. It is a free citation taken from Is. 54,13: "And they shall all be taught by God." (v. 45) This saying corresponds to Jesus' own, primary teaching that it is the Father who gives the true bread from heaven. Thus the statement which is found in v. 27 that the Son of Man gives the eternal food takes on a new meaning.

The Prophet

It is none other than the very God of Israel who gives Jesus, the Incarnate Son and the Son of Man, as spiritual food for the world.

Jesus is not only another prophet like Ezekiel and Moses. As the incarnate Logos he is also the eternal Son who has come down from heaven who has been sent from the Father. It is because of this event that he is thus also the Son of Man who is the very incarnation of the true bread from heaven. He is the supreme prophet, the Hebrew God incarnate, who has taken on human form. It is this fact alone which enables 6,53 to provide a meaningful statement about Jesus' character and which finally clarifies his true nature in a complete and thoroughgoing manner. It is the essential nature of Jesus, the Father, and the Son of Man that they are all one. The saying of John 6,53 is ultimately valid because of this unique oneness. It is only this oneness which, as Moloney points out, gives rise to the central theme of the discourse and makes the belief in Jesus, the one whom the Father has sent, so crucial for the understanding of Jesus' teaching. It is for this reason that he declares, "Truly, truly, I say to you, unless you eat the flesh of the Son of Man and drink his blood, you have no life in you."

B Cullmann's Heavenly Man

Perhaps no one has better understood the consequence which follows as a result of the appearance of the Son of Man title in the sayings of Jesus than Oscar Cullmann. Contending that it is this title alone which most comprehensively "embraces the total work of Jesus,"[87] he radically suggests that a modern Christology should be founded on the New Testament Son of Man concept. He asserts that the significance which Jesus attributed to the title would thus come fully into view, whereby the great Christological debates of the 4th and 5th centuries concerning the two natures of Christ could be addressed on one level, "wo die Loesung sichtbar wird: der praeexistente Menschensohn, der im Uranfang schon bei Gott ist, mit ihm als sein Ebenbild gegeben ist, ist seinem Wesen nach schon goettlicher Mensch, so dass die ganze muehsame Diskussion, wie sie die fruehen christologischen Kaempfe beherrschte, eigentlich ueberfluessig wird."[88]

Cullmann derives his understanding of the Son of Man concept not only from the realms of apocalyptic and marginal Judaism but also from the mythology of the primal Original and Heavenly Man of the Ancient Near East, which he maintains has surfaced in a dramatic manner in the works of I Enoch, Daniel, and IV Ezra. He points to a definite influence of the Heavenly Man concept in the writings of heterodox, esoteric, and marginal Judaism as well as Jewish Christianity, and he contends that these texts must have had a corresponding impact on Jesus' determination of his own messianic mission. Consequently, he attributes to Jesus' own initiative the major, exegetical task of reconciling future and realized Son of Man eschatology, development of the claims to incarnation and pre-existence, and the identification of the Son of Man with the suffering Servant of Second Isaiah. Once this feat is accomplished, Cullmann's Son of Man functions very much like the prophetic Son of Man described above. This is particularly true of his assessment of the Johannine Son of Man, who impresses him most emphatically as one who is constantly aware of both his human and divine natures and who is supremely exalted and glorified despite the ordeal of suffering and humiliation.

Essentially Cullmann has taken the theory that the title Son of Man has been derived from apocalyptic Judaism to its logical conclusion. Convinced that the term is directly related to the concept of the divine Heavenly Man, he must first explain the phenomenon of its sudden appearance in the texts of marginal Judaism after centuries of apparent absence

The Prophet

from the Jewish milieu. At this point he must deal with the fact that there is no direct, objective, literary evidence in the annals of Judaism which substantiates what is seemingly an obvious connection to the extra-Jewish Heavenly Man, "the pre-existent heavenly being who lives in heaven from the very beginning of time until he comes to earth at the end of time."[89] Nevertheless, he is convinced that the Heavenly Man and the apocalyptic Son of Man are interchangeable concepts because of the "inexplicable fact that the eschatological redeemer is called 'man,'"[90] and because it is his opinion that the argument of silence is proof that there must have been a connection to the non-Jewish figure.

One might object to Cullmann's resolve to equate bar nasha and anthropos. Certainly if there is any equivalency between bar nasha and ben adam, then it appears that even in official, mainstream Judaism there was a tradition which supported a distinction to the generic term adam. As pointed out above, the term ben adam appears in Psalms, Ezekiel, and Daniel in a non-apocalyptic setting.

Cullmann accounts for the silence by maintaining that official Judaism was totally incapable of making a clear distinction between the concept of the eschatological figure on the one hand and the idea of the perfect, first Original Man on the other. He concludes that this is true precisely because the first man of Judaism sinned and thus forfeited completely the original, divine nature. Nevertheless, Cullmann does not rule out the possibility of a relationship between the concept of the Original Man and the first man of Judaism. Actually, he asserts that there must have been some influence, particularly since the doctrine of the Original Man was widespread and became a common feature of the religions of the Ancient Near East. Here the matter is somewhat obscured by the fact that Cullmann draws a sharp line of distinction between the Heavenly Man and the Original Man, and yet maintains that only Judaism did not succeed in combining the two concepts. However, he finds a definite parallel between the Jewish doctrine of the image of God in humankind and the concept of the divine Original Man. With respect to this development he points to the rise of the Adam literature in the realm of mainstream Judaism as well as within the marginal sphere of the apocryphal and rabbinical-mystical writings. Yet because of the sin of Adam, he concludes that the concept of the Heavenly Man must necessarily have developed in esoteric, marginal Judaism.

Therefore, the debate concerning the extra-Jewish Heavenly Man took place within marginal and apocalyptic Judaism well over a century before Jesus' day. Here the Heavenly Man and the Original Man were united and identified with the expectation that it is the heavenly ruler who has existed in heaven from the beginning of time who comes to earth at the end of time to redeem humankind. Since it has been assumed that the Jewish doctrine of representation played a role, it is maintained that the individual figure first symbolized the nation Israel. Yet according to Cullmann by the beginning of the first century A.D., the heavenly Redeemer had come to be conceptualized as a single figure.

By far the most striking and characteristic feature of the heterodox and marginal Jewish writings which presented the Heavenly Man concept was a new image of the first man Adam. The Book of I Enoch rejects the expectation of official Judaism for a political Messiah in favor of the supernatural Heavenly Man and carefully avoids developing a relationship between this figure and Adam. An account of original sin is presented which blatantly refuses to mention the Genesis story and Adam's role. Here the Son of Man concept is used extensively without relating it to the universal idea of the Original Man, a fact which might well reflect on the question of the validity of Cullmann's theory. Why would the author refuse to equate the two, particularly if he has taken such great care not to present Adam as the traditional transgressor of God's will?

One might object that the identification of Adam with sin was a foregone conclusion, so that any reference to the contrary would have been a misunderstanding. Yet the Pseudo-Clementine <u>Preaching of Peter</u>, a gnostic Jewish-Christian work, explicitly rejects the account of Adam's sin and proclaims him to be the embodiment of good! Cullmann uses this document to point up the validity of his claim that sectarian Jews comprehensively united Adam, the Origianl Man, and the Heavenly Man into the concept of a single figure. However, the Pseudo-Clementine <u>Preaching of Peter</u> not only identifies Jesus as Adam, it also understands him to be the True Prophet, who has appeared not in accordance with the Hebrew promise of the coming of the end of time, but rather with "a return of the primeval age,"[91] an expectation which is related to the Greek conception of cyclical history.

Finally, Cullmann turns to Philo to point to another manifestation of the Heavenly Man in marginal Judaism. Philo avails himself of the use of allegorical exposition of the two accounts of the creation of Adam to posit the existence of two Adams. By doing so he can describe the existence of a perfect, first man, Original Man, who is the prototype of the ideal man, as well as an ideal state of being which is attainable by means of the divine attributes given by God through the fullness of the Holy Spirit. The other Adam is carnal man who has turned from the image of God to embrace only the limited, earthly realm. He is sinful man because he was formed from the dust of the earth and does not partake fully of the divine nature. Cullmann asserts that the concept of Philo's Original Man runs parallel to that of the Heavenly Man, although this theory can be questioned. As he himself admits, the figure of the first Adam has been developed along definite Greek lines of the spiritual man who from the beginning of time partakes of absolute, divine being. The concepts of redemption and salvation by means of new divine action, incarnation, as well as an eschatological return are completely lacking.

Thus Cullmann is unable to document a consistent, uniform concept of the Heavenly Man in the writings of marginal Judaism. These texts do not reveal unanimity regarding the exact role and function of this figure. Certainly the Pseudo-Clementine <u>Preaching of Peter</u> appears to derive a more important role for Jesus taken from the Jewish expectation of the final True Prophet rather than from a functional equivalency to the figure Adam, who is regarded as the first divine man. The fact that the author of I Enoch refuses to identify the heavenly Son of Man directly with the figure of the Original Man lends support to the possible arguments either that he is aware that the Son of Man term has been taken from a Jewish source or that he has been guided by a visionary tradition which is only indirectly related to that of the Heavenly Man. With regard to Philo, it can be stated that he is most definitely working with a Greek tradition of the Man. These results point to the conclusion reached above that there was no consistent, unified concept of the Heavenly Man in apocalyptic and marginal Judaism.

Nevertheless, Cullmann is most correct in asserting that it is the general image and motif of this figure which is fundamentally operative in these and other such texts of marginal Judaism, and that it is precisely the figure of the Original Man of the religions of the Ancient Near East which has given rise to such speculation. One wonders, however, if the doctrine of original sin played such a decisive role in excluding the concept from the realm of Judaism. Could it not be that the motif of the Original Man entered the Jewish tradition at a very early date? There it was remolded and given a definite Hebrew cast according

The Prophet

to the dictates of the Hebrew view of the relationship which exists between God and humankind. Thereafter, it would have been preserved and nurtured by the ancient debate between mainstream, official Judaism on the one hand, and the tradition of the Hebrew prophets on the other.

Most scholars agree that the author or authors of the Hebrew account of the first man and woman did not intend for that story to be understood literally. Cullmann has rightly observed that no saying has been preserved which records Jesus' interpretation of that account or any comment of his related to it. Jesus appears to document the beginning of Judaism with the story of Abraham and Sarah. Could this fact itself perhaps be an indirect interpretation of the Adam story?

It is at least likely that the first Hebrews did not believe that there had once been a paradise on earth. The primary thrust of the story points to the acknowledgment of a single God, whom one is compelled to recognize, honor, and obey, as well as the awareness of a spiritual realm beyond the material, earthly domain which is ruled omnipotently and omnisciently by this God. The central aim of the story is to symbolically depict the real, true, and essential predicament of humankind. When one views the matter from this perspective, the concept of sin is not paramount. Far more important is the Hebrew axiom that humankind is redeemed by means of the acknowledgment of and the abiding obedience to one, particular God.

As the image of the first, divine Original Man was likely regarded by non-Hebrews of the Ancient Near East to be the source of their "own" divinity, so also in a similar manner might the Hebrews themselves have envisioned the idea of the image of God residing within the individual. Yet because they became acutely aware of the distinct, personal, and divine character of this God with whom they could personally communicate via dreams and visions, they could never conceive of the individual as an equivalent source of righteousness and divinity. The first man Adam sinned when he thought that he could attain a specific knowledge which would make him the sole master of his own fate; and yet it is precisely this attempt which grants him the true vision and understanding of the Hebrew God. Only on this condition of mutual exclusion, therefore, did the perfect, celestial, divine Original Man come to dwell paradoxically within the Hebrew soul.

Because the story of Adam's redemption is essentially the same as that of Abraham, Jesus could well have referred indirectly to it when he spoke of Abraham and the beginning of the Israelite nation. There might well have been other Abrahams for whom there are no records, but whose prototype would have been that of Adam. By pointing specifically to Abraham, Jesus was referring to a distinct, definite, historical figure who was known to the Hebrew nation as its founder.

It is this same understanding of redemption which is preserved and documented throughout the writings of the Hebrew prophets. Each prophecy begins either with a brief or elaborate account of the manner in which the prophet was made aware of and apprehended the majestic presence of the Hebrew God. Thereafter, the individuality and personal talents of the prophet are offered up to the dictates of the one God, who demands such a sacrifice to provide for the redemption of individual and corporate humanity as well as the fulfillment of God's will.

Cullmann concedes that there are several disadvantages for assuming that the Son of Man who appears in the sayings of Jesus is the Heavenly Man of apocalyptic and marginal Judaism. Foremost among these is the concept of incarnation. It is quite clear that the apocalyptic Heavenly Man is a pre-existent, heavenly being who descends to earth only at the end of time and who bears only the resemblance of a man. Since this figure does not take on human form and does not reside on earth, he is also

The Prophet

totally incapable of suffering. Cullmann has assumed that Jesus' perfect, divine, messianic nature empowered him with the authority to make a claim for incarnation and to combine the role of the Heavenly Man with that of the suffering Servant of Second Isaiah. Yet this is not only problematic from the particular, eschatological nature of the apocalyptic Son of Man, it also has consequences with regard to the role of the eschatological judge, a role which Jesus emphatically assigns to himself. Certainly, Jesus cannot have pretended to assume the role of the heavenly judge at the end of time who is depicted in I Enoch. As has been concluded above, his authority to judge is directly related to the fact of the incarnation. He is an authoritative judge on earth because he has taken on human form.

Thus Jesus' understanding of the role of the Son of Man emphasizes the manifestation of the element of the divine within the human sphere and appears to result paradoxically from the awareness that, although he has taken on human form, he is nonetheless his true, divine, original self. Because the movement is most definitely from the human sphere to that of the divine realm, the role of the final True Prophet is most appropriately related to the mission which Jesus came to accomplish on earth. Cullmann has considered this option, and yet has ruled it out because it does not describe in a comprehensive manner the complete earthly work of Jesus; a delay of the expected, impending Kingdom of God; the future, eschatological phase of the church; the vicarious suffering of the eschatological prophet; and the concept of pre-existence. He admits, however, that the function of the prophet has numerous advantages for depicting Jesus' role as the Messiah, and even asserts on several occasions that it is the concept of the Prophet which best allows for the expectation of a second coming of Jesus to earth.[92]

Both mainstream and marginal Judaism expected the eschatological

Prophet to appear as a man on earth to announce with full and final, divine authority the coming of the Kingdom of God. Since this expectation was centered on a man who was to appear as a prophet, it can be assumed that it was expected of him that he suffer and be rejected, as that was the common fate of most all Hebrew prophets. Yet as Cullmann indicates, there are quite a number of varied expectations regarding the role of the Prophet, one of which involves the return of a former prophet as the eschatological prophet. One is reminded of the dilemma which was encountered with the attempt to delineate a definite role for the Heavenly Man. Here a similar conclusion must perhaps be reached. Just as there is no single, unifying concept of the apocalyptic Man, so also there is no consistent, precise, unified expectation for the final True Prophet which can be documented within mainstream as well as marginal Judaism.

The pre-existent, apocalyptic Heavenly Man is no better suited for the role Jesus ascribes to his concept of the Son of Man than is the eschatological Prophet. Just as one must struggle to explain the delay of the coming of the Kingdom of God by means of a final, eschatological event after the appearance of Jesus as the Prophet, so must one labor to account for the delay of the final judgment and the end of time anticipated with the advent of the Heavenly Man. It must be pointed out here that the coming of the Mosaic Prophet which is prophesied in Deut. 18,15ff does not include such a specific, eschatological expectancy. The function of this figure is summed up with these words: "... him you shall heed." The coming of this prophet is coupled with the final command of v. 18: "I will raise up for them a prophet like you from among their brethren; and I will put my words in his mouth, and he shall speak to them all that I command him." Finally, it can be noted that it is more convenient to relate the role of a suffering Messiah to that of a

The Prophet

suffering prophet whose divine mission has been ignored because he has appeared as a human on earth than to that of a pre-existent, heavenly being.

Cullmann has rightly observed that it is the Evangelist of the Gospel of John who appears to reserve for Jesus the title, Mosaic Prophet. Yet it is also true that no saying, not even one of the Synoptic logia, reports Jesus' direct claim to this title. The Gospel of John is unique in that it is the only gospel which reports that Jesus directly asserted that he was both the Messiah and the Son of Man. Since it is clear, however, that the Evangelist does not regard John the Baptist as the final, eschatological Prophet, it seems certain that he understands Jesus to be the Prophet in the sense that he is considered to be the Mosaic Prophet. Furthermore, it is evident that Jesus himself was aware of the complexity of the numerous expectations regarding the Prophet and the Messiah, and that he knew that he had not come to fulfill the popular, traditional expectations related to either of these figures. Yet not only in chapter 9 but throughout the Gospel of John, the Evangelist records Jesus' emphatic pronouncement that he is the Son of Man. Can it not be, therefore, that it is in this manner that Jesus sought to interpret and define the roles of the Hebrew Messiah and Mosaic Prophet? This is to conclude that as the Son of Man he fulfills these roles to the extent that he is the very embodiment of the Hebrew God who has spoken to Israel through the prophets throughtout the ages, and that he himself has appeared on earth as one of the suffering prophets.

Cullmann asserts that the Gospel of John has preserved a unique understanding of the concept of the Son of Man. He has rightly observed that the motifs of exaltation and glorification are intricately interwoven with the themes of revelation and suffering; and he has very successfully distinguished between the Synoptic picture of the Son of Man as one who suffers in the present and is exalted in the future, and the Johannine panorama of pre-existence and eschatological judgment focused on a present moment of the Son of Man's glory.

It cannot be denied that Cullmann is thoroughly justified in his attempt to locate the Johannine community in a milieu closely related to esoteric and marginal Judaism. His assertion that the Judean segment of the Johannine community as well as the "Hellenists" of the Book of Acts are to be viewed as groups similar to the community at Qumran or the marginal group which produced the Book of Enoch has considerable merit. There can be no doubt about the fact that the Gospel of John was produced in an environment where criticism of official, mainstream Judaism was extremely pronounced. As has been indicated above, however, it cannot be assumed that the Johannine Son of Man is directly related to the apocalyptic figure. Above all, the prophetic nature of the Johannine Jesus reveals most emphatically that the Johannine community occupied a definite middle ground between mainstream Judaism and the marginal groups, and yet despite that fact it was more closely related to the former than the latter.

IV Conclusion

It must be concluded, therefore, that the term Son of Man does not function as an apocalyptic title in the Gospel of John. There is no evidence within the Gospel itself which supports the theory that the Evangelist has patterned his use of the term on the Danielic concept of the transcendent Redeemer, the celestial Son of Man of I Enoch, or the Man who rises from the sea in IV Ezra. Not only is there a marked absence of apocalyptic imagery in the Gospel, the Evangelist's use of the title betrays a definite theological purpose which is determined by the unique revelatory status of Jesus. Jesus is God's unique Messiah who has appeared in the course of time and history in accordance with the prophecy of Moses and the prophets. He is not a transcendent, apocalyptic Son of Man who flies on the clouds and who is enthroned on the throne of God before the heavenly court. There is also evidence to support the view that Jesus himself consciously rejected the apocalyptic expectations of his day. John's presentation of Jesus in chapter 5 as the giver of life and the eschatological judge is painted against the background of traditional, Jewish eschatology, not the extravagant, apocalyptic description of the end of time.

This does not mean that the term Son of Man in John does not function as a messianic title. There is every indication that it does. However, the Evangelist has fashioned its use as a messianic title on a concept other than that of the transcendent figure of Jewish apocalyptic literature. Since the title occurs often in a midrashic discussion which points to an interdependency between it and the concept of the

Conclusion

Mosaic-Prophet-Messiah, it is highly likely that the Evangelist has derived his use of the term as a messianic title from a prophetic background and tradition. In this light the poetic use of the term in the Psalms and its use as a means of address in Ezekiel take on a renewed significance. Also the appearance of the term in the Jewish-Christian, apocryphal work, The Testament of Abraham, points to a similar usage. It is, therefore, highly probable that the term Son of Man was a somewhat obscure yet significant phrase which provided a means of referring to prophetic office. It served to indicate the divine presence which had made itself manifest to the human prophet.

The function ascribed to the term Son of Man as a messianic title in the Gospel of John points to this usage. The Son of Man is God's unique revealer on earth. In his study of the thirteen logia in John, Moloney has found that it is as the Son of Man that Jesus performs his revelatory role on earth. It is as the Incarnate Son, the Son of Man, that Jesus serves as the place on earth where God is revealed to humankind. Divine revelation is thus transmitted through a human element to all humankind. After the crucifixion the title, Son of Man, is quietly discarded by the Evangelist, since Jesus is no longer present in the earthly realm in a human body. The importance of the suffering Servant of Second Isaiah cannot be overlooked here. Not only does the particularly Johannine use of the verb, ὑψωθῆναι, coincide with Is. 52,13("Behold, my servant shall prosper, he shall be exalted and lifted up, and shall be very high."), it is the suffering Johannine Jesus who brings revelation to the world via the climax of the cross.

It is well-known that there were a number of conflicting messianic expectations current in Jesus' day. The Evangelist has clearly opted for the Mosaic-Prophet-Messiah, although he has vigorously rejected the notion that he was to reign as a political king. The Jewish apocalyptic

Conclusion

literature and other marginal works such as The Testament of Abraham seek primarily to present other variations of messianic expectation. Although The Testament of Abraham is not an apocalyptic work, it too preserves a prophecy about the day of judgment. "This one is the son of Adam, the first created one, who is called Abel, whom the evil Cain killed. Now he is seated here to judge all creation and to bring to light who is righteous and who is a sinner. This is why God has said: 'I do not judge you, but every human being is judged by a human being.'" (Test. Abr. A 12-13) There can be little doubt that Jesus was responding to messianic expectations current during his day as well as prophecies about the day of judgment and the one appointed to judge when he uttered the words of John 5,27. According to the testimony of this chapter and the Evangelist's use of the Son of Man title throughout the Gospel, it is clear that as he did so, he made a conscious effort to respect the distinct tradition of the Hebrew prophetic heritage and to faithfully represent the corresponding, Israelite, eschatological expectations which had been developed by the prophets during the course of the history of the Hebrew people.

Notes to the Text

[1] Reginald H. Fuller, "The Son of Man: A Reconsideration," p. 207.

[2] Eduard Schweizer, "The Son of Man," JBL, p. 119.

[3] I. H. Marshall, "The Synoptic Son of Man Sayings," p. 329.

[4] Ibid., p. 332.

[5] Ibid., p. 333.

[6] Ibid.

[7] Ibid., p. 331.

[8] Eduard Schweizer, "Der Menschensohn," ZNW, p. 203.

[9] Carsten Colpe, "Uios tou anthropou," pp. 400-477.

[10] Norman Perrin, "The Son of Man," p. 20.

[11] Ibid., pp. 17-28.

[12] Ragnar Leivestad, "Der Apokalyptische Menschensohn," pp. 49-105.

[13] Reginald H. Fuller, "The Son of Man: A Reconsideration," pp. 207-217.

[14] Barnabas Lindars, Jesus Son of Man, p. 27.

[15] Ibid., pp. 1-189.

[16] Francis J. Moloney, The Johannine Son of Man, p. 11.

[17] Rudolf Otto, The Kingdom of God and the Son of Man, p. 236.

[18] Carsten Colpe, "Uios tou anthropou," p. 419.

[19] Ibid.

[20] Matthew Black, "Jesus and the Son of Man," p. 15.

[21] Ibid., p. 13.

[22] Ibid., p. 12.

[23] Ibid., p. 15.

[24] Ibid., p. 13.

[25] Ibid.

Notes to the Text

[26] J. A. Emerton, "The Origin of the Son of Man Imagery," p. 228.

[27] James Muilenburg, "The Son of Man," p. 207.

[28] M. D. Hooker, The Son of Man in Mark, p. 49.

[29] Ibid., p. 47.

[30] F. H. Borsch, The Son of Man in Myth and History, p. 132.

[31] Ibid., p. 145.

[32] Ibid., p. 154.

[33] Ibid.

[34] Stephen S. Smalley, "The Johannine Son of Man Sayings," p. 287.

[35] Ibid., p. 298.

[36] J. L. Martyn, History and Theology in the Fourth Gospel, p. 139.

[37] Raymond E. Brown, The Gospel According to John, Vol. I, p. 218.

[38] Ibid.

[39] Ibid., p. 220.

[40] Francis J. Moloney, The Johannine Son of Man, p. 74.

[41] Raymond E. Brown, The Gospel According to John, Vol. I, p. 220.

[42] Francis J. Moloney, The Johannine Son of Man, p. 74.

[43] Ibid., p. 84.

[44] Rudolf Schnackenburg, The Gospel According to St. John, Vol. I, pp, 114-119.

[45] Francis J. Moloney, The Johannine Son of Man, p. 120.

[46] Raymond E. Brown, The Gospel According to John, Vol. I, p. 296.

[47] C. K. Barrett, The Gospel According to St. John, p. 303.

[48] Ibid.

[49] F. H. Borsch, The Son of Man in Myth and History, p. 301.

[50] Raymond E. Brown, The Gospel According to John, Vol. I, p. 300.

[51] Francis J. Moloney, The Johannine Son of Man, p. 122.

[52] Raymond E. Brown, The Gospel According to John, Vol. I, p. 299.

[53] Ibid., p. 300.

Notes to the Text

[54] Ibid.

[55] Francis J. Moloney, The Johannine Son of Man, p. 120.

[56] Ibid., p. 122.

[57] Ibid., p. 123.

[58] Ibid.

[59] Ibid.

[60] J. L. Martyn, History and Theology in the Fourth Gospel, p. 140.

[61] Francis J. Moloney, The Johannine Son of Man, p. 144.

[62] Raymond E. Brown, The Gospel According to John, Vol. I, p. 381.

[63] J. L. Martyn, History and Theology in the Fourth Gospel, pp. 102-128.

[64] Stephen S. Smalley, "The Johannine Son of Man Sayings," p. 296.

[65] F. H. Borsch, The Son of Man in Myth and History, p. 305.

[66] Francis J. Moloney, The Johannine Son of Man, p. 158.

[67] Raymond E. Brown, The Gospel According to John, Vol. I, p. 381.

[68] Francis J. Moloney, The Johannine Son of Man, p. 152.

[69] Ragnar Leivestad, "Der Apokalyptische Menschensohn," p. 63.

[70] Raymond E. Brown, The Gospel According to John, Vol. I, p. 375.

[71] F. H. Borsch, The Son of Man in Myth and History, p. 295.

[72] Ibid., p. 297.

[73] C. H. Dodd, The Interpretation of the Fourth Gospel, pp. 333-334; 344-345.

[74] Rudolf Bultmann, Das Evangelium des Johannes, pp. 173-176.

[75] Raymond E. Brown, The Gospel According to John, Vol. I, p. 286.

[76] Ibid., p. 287.

[77] Francis J. Moloney, The Johannine Son of Man, p. 98.

[78] Ibid., p. 100.

[79] Ibid., p. 99.

[80] Peder Borgen, Bread from Heaven, p. 59.

[81] Ibid., pp. 80-97.

Notes to the Text

[82] Francis J. Moloney, <u>The Johannine Son of Man</u>, p. 104.

[83] Raymond E. Brown, <u>The Gospel According to John</u>, Vol. I, p. 273.

[84] Francis J. Moloney, <u>The Johannine Son of Man</u>, p. 119.

[85] Ibid.

[86] Raymond E. Brown, <u>The Gospel According to John</u>, Vol. I, p. 261.

[87] Oscar Cullmann, <u>The Christology of the New Testament</u>, p. 137.

[88] Oscar Cullmann, <u>Die Christologie des Neuen Testaments</u>, p. 198.

[89] Oscar Cullmann, <u>The Christology of the New Testament</u>, p. 142.

[90] Ibid., p. 144.

[91] Ibid., p. 148.

[92] Ibid., p. 43.

Bibliography

Barrett, C. K. The Gospel According to St. John. Philadelphia: The Westminster Press, 1978.

Barrett, C. K. The Gospel of John and Judaism. London: SPCK, 1975.

Black, Matthew. "Jesus and the Son of Man." Journal for the Study of the New Testament. Vol. I. Sheffield, 1978.

Borgen, Peder. Bread from Heaven. Supplements to Novum Testamentum. 10. Leiden: E. J. Brill, 1965.

Borsch, Frederick H. The Son of Man in Myth and History. London: SCM Press, 1967.

Bousset, Wilhelm. Die Religion des Judentums. Berlin: Verlag von Reutner und Reichard, 1903.

Bowker, J. W. "The Origin and Purpose of St. John's Gospel." New Testament Studies. Vol. 11. Cambridge: At the University Press, 1959-1960. pp. 398-408.

Brown, J. P. "The Son of Man: 'This Fellow.'" Biblica. Vol. 58. Rome, 1977. pp. 361-387.

Brown, Raymond E. The Gospel According to John. The Anchor Bible Series. Vols. I & II. Garden City, New York: Doubleday and Company Inc., 1966.

Bultmann, Rudolf. Das Evangelium des Johannes. 12 Auflage. Goettingen: Vandenhoeck und Ruprecht, 1952.

Colpe, Carsten. "Uios tou anthropou." The Theological Dictionary of the New Testament. Vol. 8. Grand Rapids: Wm. B. Eerdmans Publishing Company, 1972. pp. 400-477.

Cullmann, Oscar. Early Christian Worship. Translated by A. S. Todd and J. B. Torrance. London: SCM Press LTD, 1953.

Cullmann, Oscar. Der johanneische Kreis. Tuebingen: J. C. B. Mohr (Paul Siebeck), 1975.

Cullmann, Oscar. Die Christologie des Neuen Testaments. Tuebingen: J. C. B. Mohr (Paul Siebeck), 1957.

Cullmann, Oscar. The Christology of the New Testament. Translated by S. C. Guthrie and C. A. M. Hall. Philadelphia: The Westminster Press, 1959.

Bibliography

Danielou, Jean. The Theology of Jewish Christianity. Translated and edited by John A. Baker. London: Darton, Longmann & Todd, 1964.

Dodd, C. H. The Interpretation of the Fourth Gospel. Cambridge: At the University Press, 1953.

Emerton, J. A. "The Origin of the Son of Man Imagery." Journal of Theological Studies. (new series) Vol. 9. Oxford: 1958. pp. 225-242.

Freed, E. D. "The Son of Man in the Fourth Gospel." The Journal of Biblical Literature. Vol. 86. Philadelphia, 1967. pp. 402-409.

Fuller, Reginald H. "The Son of Man: A Reconsideration." The Living Text: Essays in Honor of Ernest W. Saunders. Lantham, MD.: The University Press of America, 1985.

Hamerton-Kelley. Pre-existence, Wisdom, and the Son of Man. Cambridge: At the University Press, 1973.

Higgins, A. J. B. Jesus and the Son of Man. London: Lutterworth, 1964.

Hindley, J. C. "Towards a Date for the Similitudes of Enoch." New Testament Studies. Vol. 14. Cambridge: At the University Press, 1973.

Hooker, M. D. The Son of Man in Mark. Montreal: McGill University Press, 1967.

Jeremias, J. "Die aelteste Schichte der Menschensohnlogien." Zeitschrift fuer die Neutestamentliche Wissenschaft. Vol. 58. Berlin: 1967.

Kinniburgh, E. "The Johannine Son of Man." Studia Evangelica. Vol. 4. 1968. pp. 64-71.

Koch, Klaus. The Rediscovery of Apocalyptic. Studies in Biblical Theology. Second Series. 22. Naperville: Alec R. Allenson Inc., 1970.

Leivestad, Ragnar. "Der apokalyptische Menschensohn ein Phantom." Annual of the Swedish Theological Institute. Vol. 6. Jerusalem, 1968. pp. 49-105.

Leivestad, Ragnar. "Exit the Apocalyptic Son of Man." New Testament Studies. Vol. 18. Cambridge: At the University Press, 1971-1972. pp. 243-267.

Leroy, Herbert. Raetsel und Missverstaendnis. Bonn: Peter Hanstein Verlag GMBH, 1968.

Lindars, Barnabas. "The Son of Man in the Johannine Christology." Christ and Spirit in the New Testament. Edited by B. Lindars and S. S. Smalley. Cambridge: At the University Press, 1973.

Lindars, Barnabas. Jesus Son of Man. London: SPCK, 1983.

Maddox, R. "The Function of the Son of Man in the Gospel of John." Reconciliation and Hope. Edited by R. J. Banks. Exeter: Paternoster Press, 1974.

Bibliography

Manson, T. W. Studies in the Gospels and Epistles. Edited by M. Black. Manchester: The University Press, 1962.

Marshall, I. H. "The Synoptic Son of Man Sayings In Recent Discussion." New Testament Studies. Vol. 12. Cambridge: At the University Press, 1965-1966. pp. 327-351.

Martyn, J. Louis. History and Theology in the Fourth Gospel. New York: Harper & Row, 1968.

Meeks, W. A. "The Man from Heaven in Johannine Sectarianism." Journal of Biblical Literature. Vol. 91. Philadelphia, 1972. pp. 44-72.

Moloney, Francis J. The Johannine Son of Man. Biblioteca Di Scienze Religiose. 14. Rome: Libreria Ateneo Salesiano, 1976.

Morgenstern, Julian. "The Son of Man of Daniel 7,13f. A New Interpretation." Journal of Biblical Literature. Vol. 80. Philadelphia, 1961. pp. 65-77.

Muilenburg, James. "The Son of Man in Daniel and the Ethiopic Apocalypse of Enoch." Journal of Biblical Literature. Vol. 79. Philadelphia, 1960. pp. 197-209.

Otto, Rudolf. The Kingdom of God and the Son of Man. Translated by F. V. Filson and B. L. Woolf. London: Lutterworth, 1938.

Perrin, Norman. "The Son of Man in Ancient Judaism and Primitive Christianity: A Suggestion." Biblical Research. Vol. 11. Chicago, 1966. pp. 15-28.

Pollard, T. E. Johannine Christology and the Early Church. Cambridge: At the University Press, 1970.

Reim, Gunther. Studien zum alttestamentlichen Hintergrund des Johannesevangeliums. Cambridge: At the University Press, 1974.

Ricca, P. Die Eschatologie des vierten Evangeliums. Zurich: Gotthelf, 1966.

Robinson, James. The Nag Hammadi Library in English. San Francisco: Harper & Row, 1977.

Ruckstuhl, Eugen. "Abstieg und Erhohung des Johanneischen Menschensohns." Jesus und der Menschensohn. Hrsg. von R. Pesch und R. Schnackenburg. Freiburg, Basel, Wien: Verlag Herder KG, 1975. pp. 314-341.

Russell, D. S. The Method and Message of Jewish Apocalyptic. Philadelphia: The Westminster Press, 1964.

Schnackenburg, Rudolf. "Der Menschensohn im Johannesevangelium." New Testament Studies. Vol. 11. Cambridge: At the University Press, 1964-1965. pp. 213-237.

Schnackenburg, Rudolf. The Gospel According to St. John. Vol. I. Trans-

Bibliography

lated by Kevin Smith. New York: Herder & Herder, 1968.

Schoeps, Hans-Joachim. <u>Jewish Christianity</u>. Philadelphia: Fortress Press, 1969.

Schulz, Siegfried. <u>Untersuchungen zur Menschensohn-Christologie im Johannesevangelium</u>. Goettingen: Vandenhoeck und Ruprecht, 1957.

Schwank, B. "Das Johannesevangelium." <u>Die Welt der Bibel</u>. Vol. 1. Dusseldorf: Fatmos, 1966-1968. pp. 101-103.

Schweizer, Eduard. "The Son of Man." <u>Journal of Biblical Literature</u>. Vol. 79. Philadelphia, 1960. pp. 119-129.

Schweizer, Eduard. "Der Menschensohn." <u>Zeitschrift fuer die Neutestamentliche Wissenschaft</u>. Vol. 50. Berlin, 1959. pp. 185-209.

Sidebottom, E. M. <u>The Christ of the Fourth Gospel in the Light of First Century Thought</u>. London: SPCK, 1961.

Smalley, Stephen S. <u>John: Evangelist and Interpreter</u>. Exeter: The Paternoster Press, 1978.

Smalley, Stephen S. "The Johannine Son of Man Sayings." <u>New Testament Studies</u>. Vol. 15. Cambridge: At the University Press, 1968. pp. 278-301.

Smalley, Stephen S. "Johannes 1:51 und die Einleitung zum vierten Evangelium." <u>Jesus und der Menschensohn</u>. Hrsg. von R. Pesch und R. Schnackenburg. Freiburg, Basel, Wien: Verlag Herder KG, 1975. pp. 300-314.

Toedt, H. E. <u>The Son of Man in the Synoptic Tradition</u>. London: SCM Press, 1965.

Vielhauer, Philipp. <u>Aufsaetze zum Neuen Testament</u>. Muenchen: Chr. Kaiser Verlag, 1965.

Walker, Jr. W. O. "The Origin of the Son of Man Concept as Applied to Jesus." <u>Journal of Biblical Literature</u>. Vol. 91. Philadelphia, 1972. pp. 482-490.

Windisch, H. "Angelophanien um den Menschensohn auf Erden. Ein Kommentar zu Joh. 1,51." <u>Zeitschrift fuer die Neutestamentliche Wissenschaft</u>. Vol. 30. Berlin, 1931. pp. 215-233.

Young, F. W. "A Study of the Relation of Isaiah to the Fourth Gospel." <u>Zeitschrift fuer die Neutestamentliche Wissenschaft</u>. Vol. 46. Berlin, 1955.

www.ingramcontent.com/pod-product-compliance
Lightning Source LLC
Chambersburg PA
CBHW051702090426
42736CB00013B/2494